Stanton Allaben's
VERMONT SKI TRAIL GUIDE
Central Region

A CROSS-COUNTRY SKIER'S GUIDE TO TRAILS IN THE GREEN MOUNTAINS OF CENTRAL VERMONT

1983
(FIRST EDITION)
FIRST PRINTING
$5.00

PUBLISHED BY

STANTON ALLABEN PRODUCTIONS
70 LITTLE POND ROAD
LONDONDERRY, VERMONT 05148

EDITOR

STANTON ALLABEN

OTHER CROSS COUNTRY SKI TRAIL GUIDES BY STANTON ALLABEN

Vermont Ski Trail Guide - South Central Region
1982 $4.50

New Hampshire Ski Trail Guide - White Mountain Region
1983 by Denise and Thom Perkins $5.00

TO ORDER BOOKS SEND CHECK OR MONEY ORDER TO:

**Stanton Allaben Productions
70 Little Pond Road
Londonderry, Vermont 05148**

Add 50¢ per book for postage and handling.

Copyright © 1983 by
Stanton Allaben Productions
First Edition
All Rights Reserved

ISBN #0-913109-01-0

Acknowledgements

Tony Clark	Blueberry Hill, Goshen, Vermont
John Tidd	Mountain Meadows, Killington, Vermont
Don Cochrane	Mountain Top, Chittenden, Vermont
Rick Robinson	United States Forest Service
Bruce Flewelling	United States Forest Service
Rob Center	Tucker Hill, Waitsfield, Vermont
John Wiggin	Woodstock Resort, Woodstock, Vermont
Ann Mausolff	Ski Tours of Vermont, Chester, Vermont
John Welter	Waitsfield, Vermont
Dean Mendell	Nordic Adventures, Stockbridge, Vermont
Dick DeBonis	United States Forest Service
Al Stiles	Middlebury, Vermont

Vermont Fish and Game Department

CONTENTS

AREA MAP	v
ABOUT THE AUTHOR	vi
TO THE OWNER OF THIS BOOK	vii
INTRODUCTION	viii

CHAPTER

1)	Killington - Chittenden	2
2)	Woodstock - Barnard	25
3)	Lincoln - Goshen	46
4)	Rochester - Hancock	69
5)	Waitsfield - Warren	91
6)	Montpelier - Randolph	109

NATURE NOTES

White Tailed Deer	19
Fisher	108
Eastern Snow Snake	90
Eastern Coyote	44
Wild Turkey	61

GREEN MOUNTAIN NATIONAL FOREST	114
INN TO INN SKIING	116
GUIDE SERVICE	115
EMERGENCY ASSISTANCE	118
MAP RESOURCES	117
REFERENCES	117
INDEX	119

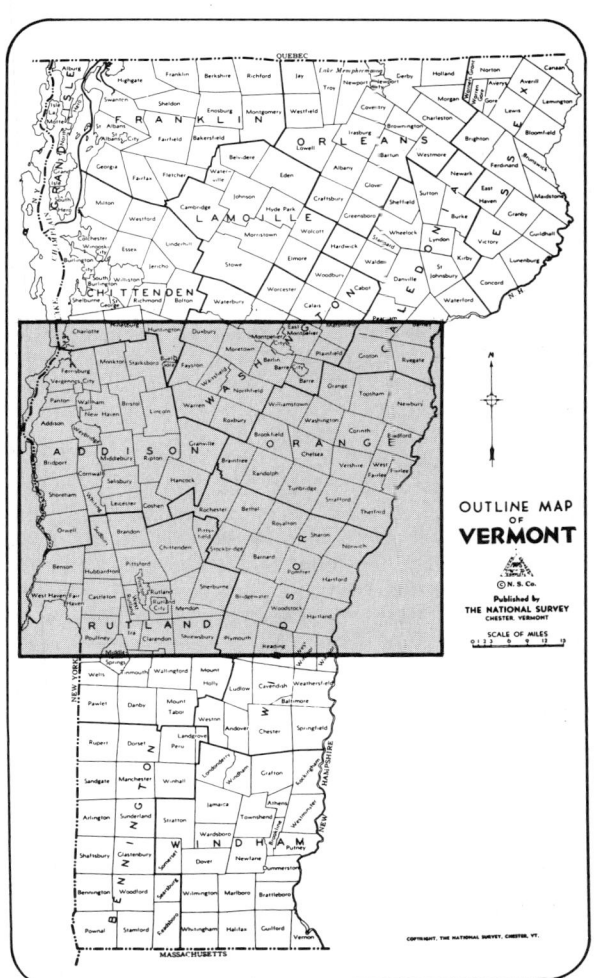

ABOUT THE AUTHOR

A native of Connecticut, Stanton Allaben moved to Vermont in 1970. With his twin brother Lee, he established the Viking Ski Touring Centre in Londonderry, one of the nation's first commercial cross country ski areas.

Stan has led numerous ski tours through the backcountry of southern Vermont, and was instrumental in establishing a 40 km. system of public trails in the Green Mountain National Forest in the Peru-Weston area near his home.

He is also a ski instructor, certified by the Professional Ski Instructors of America, and has served as a board member with the organization's Eastern division. At the same time he served four years as president of the National Ski Touring Operator's Association where he was instrumental in developing a firm rapport with the U.S. Forest Service in Washington on behalf of cross-country area operators throughout the country.

An ardent conservationist, Stan was director of the Vermont Sierra Club in the early 1970's and served on the board of directors of the Vermont Natural Resources Council, one of Vermont's most influential environmental organizations.

TO THE OWNER OF THIS BOOK

With the successful production of my first guide (Vermont Ski Trail Guide - South-Central Region) I decided that I could not stop there, but must go on and produce a total of three guides to cover all of Vermont. This, then, is the second in the series covering the central part of the state.

Because I was not as familiar with the area encompassed in this guide as with that in my first book, I found this undertaking much more challenging. I am sure there are more skiable routes out there that I missed, but they will have to wait until a second edition is begun. If you know of trails that should be included, by all means let me know where they are.

Because trail guides can be pretty dry reading, I have attempted to add a little more flavor to this production by inserting several pages of information about some of the wildlife species that inhabit this region of Vermont. You will find them scattered in the guide under the heading NATURE NOTES. As with my first book, I have also injected some historical information about the various towns in which these ski trails lie.

I wish you great enjoyment as you take this guide in hand and point your skis toward new adventures.

Göd Tur
Stanton Allaben
Editor

INTRODUCTION

Before you take this guide in hand and head for one of the trails described, there are some basic rules, and facts that you should familiarize yourself with. This knowledge can mean the difference between having a successful and enjoyable outing, or one that ends in disappointment or even disaster.

TRAIL ETIQUETTE

Good trail conditions can be degraded by unthinking and uneducated skiers. In an effort to make your skiing experience as enjoyable as possible the following "rules of the trail" are presented.

1) DO NOT WALK ON TRAILS FOR ANY REASON. Footprints degrade conditions and cause accidents. Sidestep up and down any hills you feel you can not ski.

2) FILL IN YOUR SITZMARKS. When you fall, fill in the hole you left in the snow so another skier won't catch a ski tip in it.

3) RESPECT WARNINGS AND SIGNS. Warning signs, trail markers, trail name signs, etc. are posted in many areas to aid you while skiing. Please take note of their message, and, above all, do not remove them.

4) DO NOT SKI TRAILS THAT ARE BEYOND YOUR ABILITY.

5) DO NOT SKI ALONE ON UNPATROLLED TRAILS.

6) DO NOT LITTER - CARRY OUT WHAT YOU CARRY IN.

7) DO NOT TAKE DOGS ON TRAILS. Many trails pass through deer wintering areas. Dogs are prone to chasing deer if given the opportunity. Dog tracks also degrade trail conditions.

INTRODUCTION

8) RESPECT THE RIGHTS OF OTHER USERS. (see paragraph on "Other Trail Users.")

GUIDE USE

Each trail description will include the following information:

TRAIL RATING — Each trail is rated according to degree of difficulty utilizing the rating system established by the U.S. Ski Association and the National Ski Touring Operators Association.

TYPE - Trails are categorized as to whether or not they are groomed, fee charged, marked and mapped, wilderness or forest roads.

LENGTH - Trail length is stated in kilometers (1km=.623 miles) and average time required to ski. WARNING! Times are purely estimates, and will vary with changing conditions. If you are in doubt as to your ability to complete a tour on schedule, turn back!

MAP - The name of the map required for each trail will be given. Locations where maps can be obtained are listed in the back of the guide.

ELEVATION - Two elevation figures are given for each trail - lowest and highest. This is so you can determine how much vertical climb each trail has.

OTHER TRAIL USERS

Some of the described routes are designated snowmobile trails. Be courteous to snowmobilers and give them the right of way.

Snowshoers and loggers may also be present in some areas. Any trails in the National Forest that follow designated forest roads may be open to logging operations in winter. Check with the appropriate district ranger station to see if roads are closed to skiing.

INTRODUCTION

EMERGENCIES

If, for some reason, you have need of rescue service, or medical assistance, be sure to contact the appropriate authorities immediately. A list of medical centers, and rescue services appear in the back of the guide.

Do not attempt a rescue on your own!

WARNING! Before you set off on a tour into the backcountry, let someone know what your itinerary is. Remember, "the nobody that knows you are out there is the nobody that will come looking for you."

NON-WINTER TRAIL USE

A good deal of the trails are suitable for hiking in the summer and fall. Be sure to check with the U.S. Forest Service, or appropriate local authorities for further information on use during non-winter seasons.

PRIVATE PROPERTY USE

The generosity of a large number of private property owners has made a good deal of the trails in this guide possible. As long as users are thoughtful and appreciative we will all continue to enjoy skiing across their land. Please stay on the trail and respect the landowner's rights.

PARKING

Many trail heads in this guide have very limited parking facilities. Do not block the traveled portion of any roads, as well as snowplow turnarounds.

TRAIL MEASUREMENTS

Trails are measured in kilometers. To convert to miles use this conversion chart:

1 Kilometer=.623 miles
1 mile=1.6 kilometers

INTRODUCTION

MAPS

Throughout this guide there are maps accompanying some of the specific trail descriptions, as well as general area maps to help the reader locate trail heads, and roads that lead to trail heads. Wherever contour maps are required to effectively follow a specific route, a reference to that map will be made at the beginning of the trail description.

Contour maps referred to are produced by the U.S. Forest Service (U.S.F.S.) and the U.S. Geological Survey (U.S.G.S.). Refer to the back of this guide for addresses of where maps can be obtained.

Some of the routes listed are neither marked nor mapped, and should not be skied unless you are adept at using a map and compass.

DEGREE OF DIFFICULTY

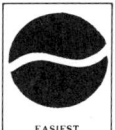
EASIEST

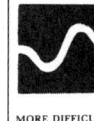
MORE DIFFICULT

MOST DIFFICULT

These national standard signs indicate relative difficulty of ski touring trails at each ski center. Remember to observe all warning signs and always ski within your ability. Be Safety Conscious!

A public service message of Cross Country Ski Areas of America

Discover Cross-country skiing.

at Art Bennett's SPORT SHOP, INC.

The most complete cross country shop in the upper valley and the original home of Ma's Sports Inc.; designer and manufacturer of custom made x-country jumping and alpine suits. *(Team prices on request).* (603) 643-6634.

Art Bennett's SPORT SHOP, INC.

24 South Main St.
Hanover, NH 03755
(603) 643-5442

CHAPTER ONE

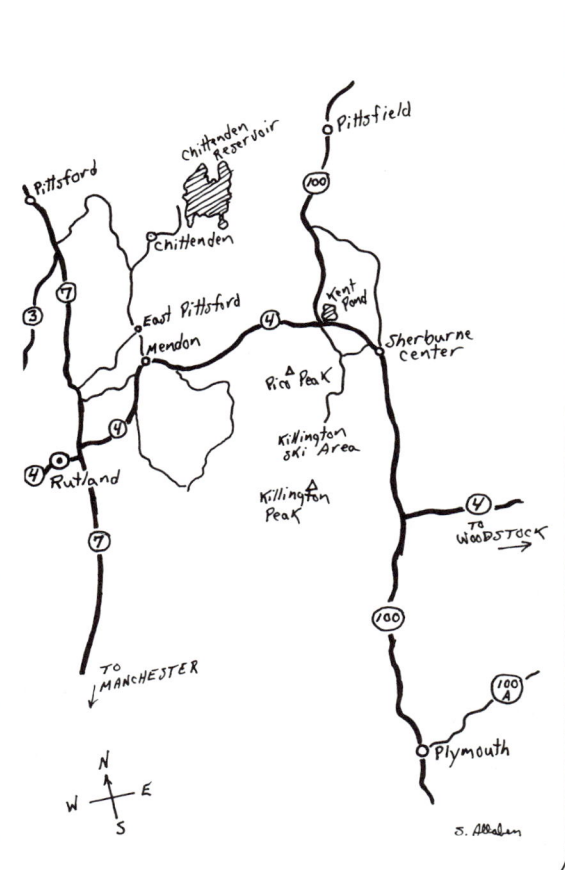

CHAPTER ONE

KILLINGTON - CHITTENDEN

The Killington - Chittenden area of central Vermont lies just east of Rutland and is very mountainous. Killington Peak is the second highest mountain in the state with an elevation of 4,241'. It is also the site of the largest commercial alpine ski area in the eastern United States. For those who enjoy telemark skiing, both Killington and Pico Peak ski areas offer great opportunities.

Besides timber production, the area's commercial activity centers on tourism. Also, in nearby Pittsfield, the Stanley Tool Company operates a wooden handle manufacturing plant.

Lodging facilities are abundant in the area with motels, lodges, and country inns situated along Route 4, the Killington access road, and in Rutland. There are movie theaters, restaurants and shops in and around Rutland, and in nearby Proctor (west of Rutland) is the Vermont Marble Exhibit, and attraction that depicts the marble industry in Vermont both past and present.

KILLINGTON-CHITTENDEN

MOUNTAIN MEADOWS SKI TOURING CENTER

RATING: **Easiest/More Difficult/Most Difficult**
TYPE: **Fee/Groomed**
MAP: **Available at the center**
ELEVATION: **1,500' - 1,800'**

Located south of the Killington ski area access road, Mountain Meadows is nestled in a beautiful high mountain valley. The touring center headquarters, which offers rental equipment, a retail shop, instruction, and food service, is attached to Mountain Meadows Lodge on one hundred acre Kent Lake.

There are 25km of groomed trails, which follow gently rolling terrain through hardwood and conifer forests and through open fields. The trail system is very well maintained and offers skiing opportunities for beginners as well as advanced skiers.

For further information write:
John Tidd
Mountain Meadows Ski Touring Center
Killington, Vermont 05751

MOUNTAIN MEADOWS S.T.C. - RECOMMENDED TRAIL - THE LONG RUN

RATING: **More Difficult**
LENGTH: **7km**

The Long Run trail starts westward from the touring center along the Appalachian Trail, which follows the edge of Lake Kent and affords nice views across the lake and down the valley. At the 1½km mark, the trail crosses Route 100 into Gifford Woods State Park where the park roadways serve as wide, groomed ski trails in the winter. Skiers pass shelters and cabins in a couple of short loops, then head north through open hardwoods to the Grey

Bonnet Inn loop, a gentle rolling trail. Branching off this is the Long Run West, which continues northward on logging roads. It is quite level for about 2km, then pitches down for a long, not-too-steep descent to Route 100 again. Across the highway (remove skis and watch the traffic) the trail is designated Long Run East and winds its way upward through mixed hemlock and hardwoods. After crossing the spillway brook there are a couple of short steeper climbs to the junction of The Perils. Here you have a choice of skiing up the Perils (only perilous in the downward direction) and back through the Orchard Trail system, or continuing on flat terrain to Kent Lake. Crossing the lake with the prevailing winds pushing from behind brings the trail full circle to the center again.

MOUNTAIN TOP SKI TOURING CENTER
RATING: **Easiest/More Difficult/Most Difficult**
TYPE: **Fee/Groomed**
MAP: **Available at the center**
ELEVATION: **1,500' - 2,000'**

When you first drive into the Mountain Top resort complex you look in awe at the incredible view to the east across the Chittenden Reservoir. The next striking feature you see is the beautiful Mountain Top Inn, rebuilt several years ago after a devastating fire destroyed the old structure. This resort complex is an impressive area indeed.

The touring center headquarters is located to the left as you drive in, up a side road just past the inn. Here there is a retail ski shop, rental shop, and cafe. Lessons by EPSIA certified instructors are offered daily. The trail system consists of 90 km, 50 of which are groomed. Lodging and restaurant facilities are available at the Mountain Top Inn.

This is one of only a handful of nordic resorts in the country that has snowmaking equipment.

For further information write:
Mountain Top Ski Touring Center
Chittenden, Vermont 05737

MOUNTAIN TOP S.T.C. - RECOMMENDED TRAIL

RATING: **Easiest/More Difficult**
LENGTH: **9 km**

The following route combines several trails in the area's complex.

Starting outside the center, ski onto Turkey Trak and follow this trail to Logger Head. From Logger Head there are nice views of the mountains to the east. This trail leads to a log cabin warming hut over rolling terrain through woodland. It then connects to the upper section of Interfield through open hardwoods and on to Red Alert. Follow Red Alert through a softwood plantation to the start of Deer Run. There is now a wide, pleasant run through open hardwoods gently downhill. This will bring you down to the Hewitt Brook Trail across two bridges and back to the center.

RUTLAND CITY FOREST

RATING: **More Difficult**
TYPE: **Logging roads**
LENGTH: **8-10 km**
MAP: **Chittenden (USFS)**
ELEVATION: **1,200' - 1,900'**

The Rutland City Forest is a watershed area located on Wheelerville Road off of Route 4 west of Pico Peak ski area. Follow Wheelerville Road approximately ¾ of a mile from Route 4. At this point the road crosses a bridge and just beyond, (before the next bridge) there is a roadway to the right. This is where you park and begin skiing.

There are several logging roads in the forest, however the main one runs southwest. The road climbs continuously and passes through a large log landing. Beyond this point the road forks, the left fork being the main route. There are some good views of Pico Peak to the east through the forest.

I have never followed any of the roads to their final destination, choosing instead, to return downhill by the same route. The downhills can be tricky, particularly where you cross several water bars across the trail.

CORTINA INN TO TULIP TREE INN

RATING: **More Difficult**
TYPE: **Roads/Snowmobile Trails**
LENGTH: **18-20 km**
TIME: **5-6 Hours**
MAP: **Chittenden and Pico Peak (USFS)**
ELEVATION: **1,300' - 2,000'**

This is a long trip, and will involve some walking since some of the roads that are followed are plowed and traveled in winter.

The trail begins behind Cortina Inn, following a nature trail. It then branches off to the left on a spur trail through open hardwoods until it connects with the Elbow Road. You will have to walk from here (to the right) until a point where the road is no longer plowed (about 2 km).

From this point the road becomes a well-defined snowmobile trail. Follow the trail along level terrain to a point where there is a summer house and a shanty on the left in a clearing. Just beyond here the trail drops sharply through a section that may be washed out and icy.

KILLINGTON-CHITTENDEN 7

The trail is very pleasant through the next section with a couple more drops until it reaches a series of beaver ponds. The beaver ponds are visible to the left. The trail goes across the beaver pond slightly to the left. On the other side is a continuation of the snowmobile trail, now heading northwest. The trail passes through lovely open hardwoods and past several summer homes. It then reaches a point where the road is plowed.

> WARNING! Do not allow your speed to pick up or you will sail over the snowbank onto gravel!

As a rule, you can ski on the road, or along the edge of the road. The route will follow the road to Lefferts Pond (on the right). Just beyond the boat access the trail crosses a swampy area and then the pond (snowmobile tracks here usually). Go due north to the far end of the pond to a stone bridge. The trail passes to the left of the bridge and up onto another road. At this point there is an option of either dropping down onto the Chittenden Reservoir and following the shore line to the left, or following a ski trail (part of Mountain Top Ski Touring Center system) over a ridge to another boat access.

> WARNING! Do not go on the reservoir unless it is solidly frozen. Also, do not follow this route if it is windy or extremely cold, as the winds tend to howl across the reservoir.

If you take the ski trail, follow the road from the stone bridge until you see the marked trail to the right. The trail climbs steeply up over the ridge and then drops steeply until it connects with an old quarry road. Go left here following the road to the boat access and out to the plowed road.

(Con't. to Page 10)

CHAPTER ONE

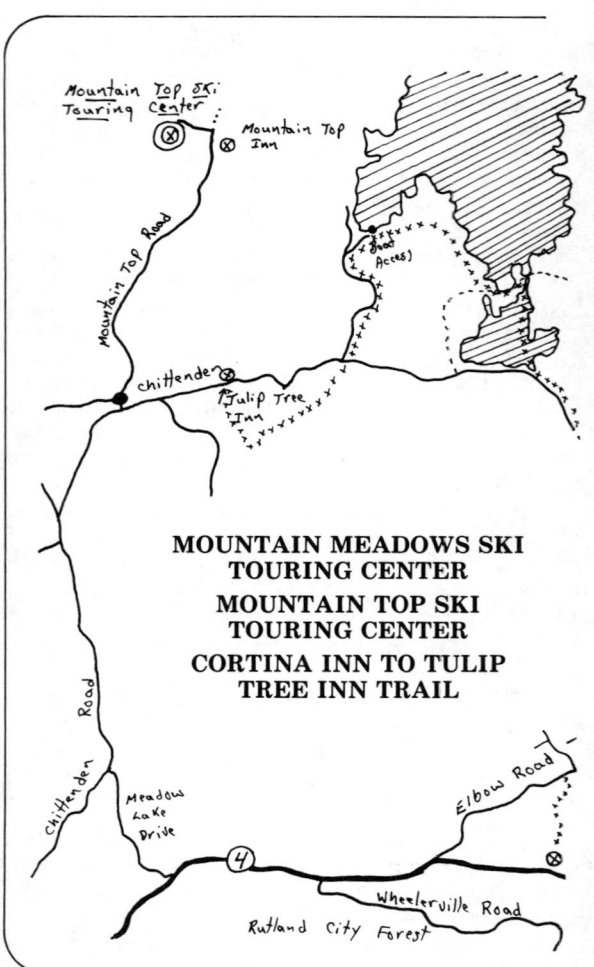

KILLINGTON-CHITTENDEN 9

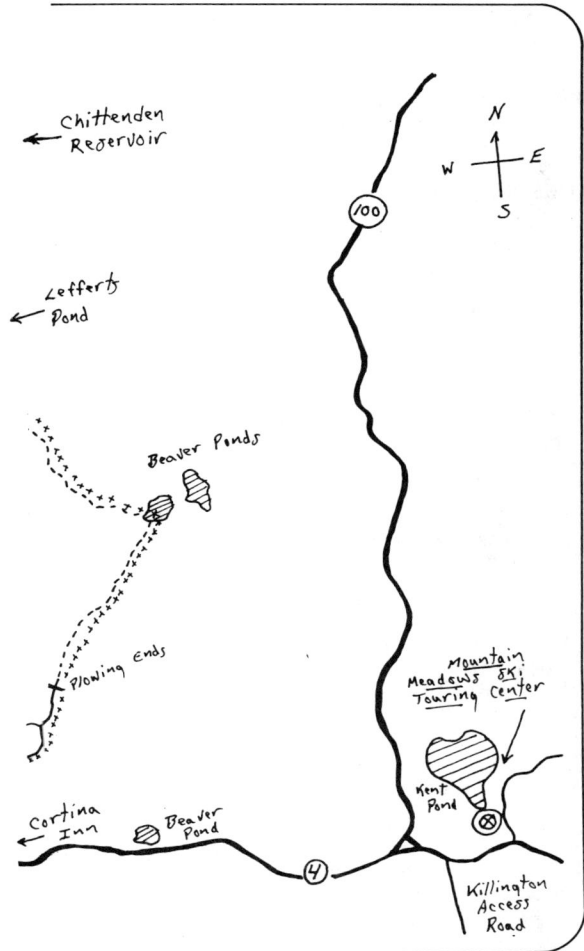

From this point you can ski down the road if there is enough snow on the side, or walk until you come to a point where a flume crosses the road. At this point the trail goes left onto a snowmobile trail. The trail is level for about 1½ km and then drops into a gorge. Use caution here as this is normally icy. Just beyond the gorge a trail cuts off to the right. Follow this down steep terrain onto an open field. Cross the field to the road and turn right. The Tulip Tree Inn is on the left.

MENDON BROOK TRAIL
RATING: **Easiest/More Difficult**
TYPE: **Marked Trail**
LENGTH: **9-10 km**
TIME: **3 Hours**
MAP: **Pico Peak and Chittenden (USFS)**
ELEVATION: **1,500' - 2,000'**

This route connects Pico Peak ski area with two inns west of Pico, the Cortina Inn and the Red Clover Inn. It can be skied from any of the three destinations as a loop. There are sections that may not be well marked, so if the route has not already been skied, you may have difficulty following it.

Beginning at Pico, the trail begins behind the Pico Bavarian Haus. Go in back of the lodge and behind the garage. Cross a clearing that lies parallel to the highway. The trail enters open hardwoods and drops immediately paralleling the brook to your right. It will then loop around to the south climbing up over a large knoll.

Coming over the knoll, the trail then drops down into a logged over area. Here it again parallels the brook and passes by a beaver pond. The countryside here is a mess as a result of a clearcut timber operation. The trail passes through this area, which is

KILLINGTON-CHITTENDEN

now overgrown with brambles. Hopefully the trail is being kept open by local skiers.

The trail passes the site of an old saw mill and then connects with the Wheelerville Road. Turn right on the road and cross the bridge. Just beyond the bridge you will see a clearly defined jeep trail to the right. Follow this road up along the brook through evergreens. It will climb gently looping left and then right again until it enters a system of trails established by the Cortina Inn. You will see a spur trail leaving the jeep road to the left. This will lead to Route 4 opposite the inn.

To get to Red Clover Inn, you will follow the Wheelerville Road west instead of taking the jeep road. Follow the road about one kilometer, crossing another bridge, until you see an old bridge on the right. Cross this and follow the road until you come to the inn.

To return to Pico from Cortina Inn, go back down the spur trail until you come to a jeep road. The trail goes left on the road to a gravel pit and then turns right dropping down to a bridge crossing the brook. Just beyond the brook the trail connects with the first section of the loop in the logged area. Go left and follow the trail back to Pico.

CHAPTER ONE

MENDON BROOK TRAIL

KILLINGTON-CHITTENDEN

PUSS AND KILL BROOK TRAIL

RATING: **More Difficult**
TYPE: **Forest Road/Trail**
LENGTH: **10 km**
TIME: **3-4 Hours**
MAP: **Mount Carmel (USFS)**
ELEVATION: **1,500' - 2,200'**

This trail runs point-to-point on a Forest Service road between Chittenden and Goshen. You will need to arrange to leave a vehicle at either end unless you feel up to a 20 km ski.

Beginning at the south end, the trail follows Forest Road 57 along Beaudry Brook. FR 57 is also known as Furnace Brook Road. The trail climbs steadily, and at times steeply through a mixture of hardwoods and evergreens. There are deer wintering areas along the route, so keep your eyes open for these forest creatures.

The trail crosses several brooks along the way. More than half way it begins its descent to Goshen. There will be some steep downhills, so use caution. The trail comes out in a small overgrown field. Go through the field and get on the driveway. Turn right and follow the driveway to the intersection of Route 73.

CHAPTER ONE

ELBOW ROAD TRAIL

RATING: **Easiest/More Difficult**
TYPE: **Town Road**
LENGTH: **7-8 km**
TIME: **2-3 Hours**
MAP: **Pico Peak (USFS)**
ELEVATION: **1,400' - 1,900'**

To find this trailhead, follow Route 100 north from Route 4 about 2¾ miles. A road goes off to the left at a sharp angle and connects back to Route 100 further north. Follow this road to an intersection of another road on the left (Stage Coach Road). Follow this left and at the fork stay left to a point where the plowing stops.

The trail begins by following the old road over very gentle terrain. It then passes through a thick conifer stand, which gives the impression of skiing through a tunnel. The trail comes upon an old farm with some apple orchards on the left.

Passing the farm, the trail climbs more steeply until it cuts through a pass between two high ridges. In this pass there is a sensational echo, so give a shout and see what happens. The trail crosses the Long Trail at this point and then drops gradually to a series of beaver ponds.

At this point you can ski back by the same route, or go on toward Chittenden Reservoir (see Cortina Inn to Tulip Tree Inn Trail - page 6). There is also the option of skiing north or south on the Long Trail.

SOUTH POND TRAIL TO ELBOW ROAD

RATING: **More Difficult/Most Difficult**
TYPE: **Forest Road/Trail/Map and Compass**
LENGTH: **8-10 km**
TIME: **3-4 Hours**
MAP: **Pico Peak (USFS)**
ELEVATION: **1,000' - 2,100'**

This route forms a loop from one trail to another and requires the use of map and compass.

Start by following the South Pond Trail (page 12) to the Long Trail. At the Long Trail go south a little over 1 km (at this point the trail will be heading southwest). From here take a compass bearing a little east of south and head downhill through open hardwoods until you connect with the Elbow Road. As long as you stay on a generally south bearing you will intersect the road somewhere. Pick the easiest route down through the woods.

When you connect with the Elbow Road turn east and follow it until you arrive at the plowed section. It is best to leave a car at either end to avoid a long walk back to the starting point.

SOUTH POND TRAIL

RATING: **More Difficult**
TYPE: **Forest Road**
LENGTH: **10 km (round trip)**
TIME: **3-4 Hours**
MAP: **Pico Peak (USFS)**
ELEVATION: **1,000' - 2,600'**

This trail begins at a point off of Route 100 about 4½ miles north of Route 4. Parking may be a problem here at times.

The trail follows an old road beginning at Route 100. It climbs steeply at the start until it reaches an

KILLINGTON-CHITTENDEN 17

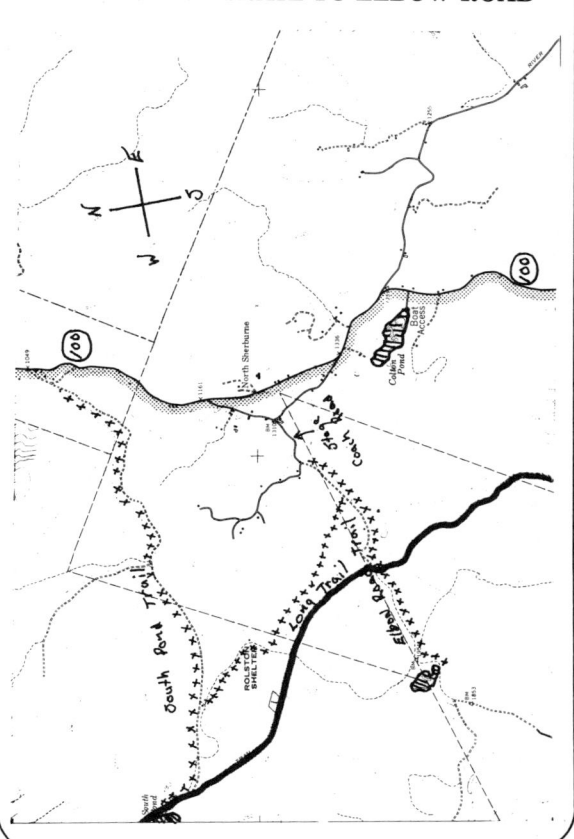

elevation of 1,400'. It then climbs more gradually along a brook down in a ravine to the right. It passes through coniferous forest at first and then into hardwoods.

The trail climbs steeply again until it reaches the 1,700' elevation. From this point the climb is more gradual and the trail crosses the brook over a bridge. Not far beyond the crossing the road forks. The right fork is a dead end. Follow the left fork climbing steeply once again.

Further on the trail intersects the Long Trail (white blazes). To the left on the Long Trail not far from the intersection is the Rolston Shelter. The main trail now climbs more gradually to the top of the ridge and then heads north to the pond. (South Pond has excellent fishing in summer). Follow the same route back using caution on the steeper downhills.

WHITETAIL DEER

WHITE TAILED DEER

Of all the wildlife species that roam the woods in winter, the white tailed deer is the one that you are most apt to see while cross-country skiing. They can most easily be found in large stands of conifer trees where they seek shelter in winter from deep snow.

Once on the brink of extinction in Vermont, the white tailed deer made a strong and steady comeback only after strict hunting laws were passed and enforced, and after a good deal of the cleared land in the state returned to forest. The changing habitat, and loss of its natural predators (wolf and mountain lion) enabled the deer to increase its numbers to such an extent that it overpopulated the land. During severe winters thousands of deer perished from starvation.

In 1979 the state permitted, by special permit, the taking of does by hunting. Before this time only bucks could be legally hunted. It is the intent of the Fish and Game Department, through this revised policy, to thin the deer population to a point that the land can support a smaller, more healthy herd, rather than a large sickly one. As of this writing the theory seems to be proving to be a valid one.

Since deer must conserve their energy in winter in order to survive, it is recommended that you disturb them as little as possible. Running through deep snow will wear a deer out very quickly. This is the primary reason that I urge skiers to leave their dogs at home when skiing in the woods.

VERMONT'S
Most Scenic Resort

Spectacular Lake & Mountain View - Warm Country Inn
Horse Drawn Sleigh Rides - Fireplaces & Fine Dining
Ice Skating, Sledding, Sauna, Whirlpool & Exercise Room

MID-WEEK SKI SPECIAL

4 Days / 3 Nights $172 Per Person, Dble. Occ., Plus Tax and Gratuity, Non Holiday Period

INCLUDES: Trail Passes, Full Breakfast & Dinner Daily
FREE use of All Facilities, Wine & Cheese Greeting
MAXI-WEEKEND AND OTHER PACKAGES AVAILABLE

1st in SKI TOURING
500 ACRES AT 2000 FEET ALTITUDE-90 km. of Trails
DAILY GROOMING - SNOW MAKING
RENTALS & LESSONS

Mountain Top Ski Touring Center

Mountain Top Inn

write Mountain Top Inn, Box 318,
Chittenden, Vt. 05737, or call TOLL FREE
1-800-445-2100. or call 1-802-483-2311.

KILLINGTON-CHITTENDEN

INN AT LONG TRAIL

The historic country inn of Killington in the heart of Vermont's best skiing. Our 22 comfortable rooms include 6 suites with fireplaces, superb dinners, hearty breakfasts, Irish Pub with Guinness on tap, hot tub. Perfect for your winter holiday.

P.O. Box 267, Rte. 4, Killington, Vt. 05751
Please call for reservations (802)775-7181

at Woodward Farm
Mendon, Vermont 05701
802-775-2290

Down a winding country road, discover a beautiful hidden mountain valley and Red Clover Inn. Charming, friendly, immaculate accommodations. Home baked breads, soups, desserts. Chef owned, just minutes from cross country trails.

The joy of skiing precise tracks
Views you can take home in your mind
Homemade soup for lunch
And friendly folks who love to ski
Come skiing with us

Mountain Meadows Ski Touring Center
13 Thundering Brook Road
Killington, Vermont 05751 (802) 775-7077

Route 4 Killington, Vermont 05751

KILLINGTON-CHITTENDEN 23

Four Diamond Award 1983

The privacy of a condominium. The services of a hotel.

Rutland's newest inn combines the luxury of a private residence with the convenience of a full-service motor hotel • Completely furnished two-bedroom, two-bath suites w/kitchen, dining area & living room • One-bedroom suites w/fully equipped kitchens • Comfortable, economical motel rooms • Panoramic views/private patios & decks • Daily maid service • Color TV, AM/FM radios

Best Western Hogge Penny Motor Inn

1-802-773-9335
P.O. Box 914B • Rutland, VT 05701
(3 miles east of Rutland on Rt. 4)
For reservations, see your travel agent or consult the Yellow Pages.

PICO BAVARIAN HAUS
(Formerly Pico Peak Lodge)
Route 4
(7 Miles east of Rutland)
Killington, VT

(802) 773-6331

Year-round resort lodge located ½ mile from Appalachian Trail, near Sherburne Pass at the entrance to the Pico Resort Alpine Slide, Killington Resort. Parklike grounds, pond, stream and bridge, lawn game area, outdoor swimming pool. Lodge with massive fireplace and balcony. Game area, restaurant and cocktail lounge. Most rooms A/C. All private baths, w/w carpeting, color TV, AAA and Mobil recommended, most major credit cards. Special rates until Sept. 15. **Hosts: Shirley and Warren Tilton.**

"Eventually everyone shows up at Charity's"

**Serving Charity's Famous French Onion Soup
Steaks, Seafood, Burgers, Salads, Quiche,
Sandwiches and Mexican plus
Daily Blackboard Specials**

Open from 11:30 a.m.
Until the legal hours.

Serving luncheon &
dinner daily.
Saturday & Sunday
Brunch 11:30.

Charitys
422-3800

A GOOD TIME EATING & DRINKING SALOON

Killington Access Road   Killington, Vermont

REAL ESTATE

FRANK PUNDERSON AGENCY

on the green
weston, vt. 05161
(802) 824-6426

8 south main street
rutland, vt. 05701
(802) 775-2552

CHAPTER TWO

WOODSTOCK - BARNARD

The village of Woodstock, in any season, is one of the prettiest and most interesting that I have ever visited. It has a rich history, and through the foresight of its citizenry, the past has been preserved magnificently.

Twenty years after Woodstock was settled (1765) it became the Shire Town, or seat of Windsor County. Culture-rich settlers immigrated from Massachusetts and Connecticut.

Throughout the 19th century the area bustled with industrial activity. Lumber and grist mills, woolen mills, a gin distillery and a brick kiln are examples of the type of industry prevalent in the area.

The earliest American breed of horse, the Morgan, was developed in Woodstock by Justin Morgan. Horseback riding is still a popular activity throughout the area.

There are three covered bridges in the area, one of which sits just west of the village green. Named the Middle Bridge, this is the first authentic covered bridge built in Vermont since 1894. Not a single nail, bolt or screw holds it together, only wooden dowels.

On the opposite side of the village green is the Woodstock Inn. The inn's history dates back to the late 1700's, when the site hosted Richardson's Tavern. By 1830 the tavern expanded and became the Eagle Hotel. In 1892 the Eagle Hotel was torn down and replaced by a tall wooden structure, which was named the Woodstock Inn.

In 1969 Laurence S. Rockefeller bought the inn, razed it, and constructed a three-story brick colonial-style hotel. It is a lovely building and well worth visiting when in the area.

The village is rich with unique shops and restaurants. Gillingham's, a fourth generation country store, is a must to visit when wandering through town.

For those with an interest in nature and conservation, a trip to the Vermont Institute of Natural Science in South Woodstock will prove to be a rewarding experience. VINS is a non-profit environmental organization with a strong emphasis on education. Lectures, field trips, bird conferences, workshops and classes are offered on a regular basis.

WOODSTOCK-BARNARD

WOODSTOCK SKI TOURING CENTER

RATING: **Easiest/More Difficult/Most Difficult**
TYPE: **Fee/Groomed**
LENGTH: **75 km**
MAP: **Available at the center**
ELEVATION: **700' - 1,100'**

The Woodstock Ski Touring Center is located on Rt. 106 just south of the village of Woodstock at the clubhouse facilities of the Woodstock Country Club. The center offers a varied trail network, from gentle golf course terrain to forest and upland pasture. It is, therefore, a wonderful area for beginners as well as the experienced skier.

Rental equipment, a full ski shop, restaurant and bar, and instruction from PSIA certified instructors are all available at the center. It is also the host area for all examinations given for instructor certification by the Professional Ski Instructors of America (PSIA) - Eastern division.

WOODSTOCK S.T.C. - RECOMMENDED TRAIL - MT. PEG

TYPE: **Groomed**
LENGTH: **7-8 km round trip**
RATING: **More Difficult**

This route is popular with skiers at the center, because its destination is the top of Mt. Peg (elevation 1,084') from which a beautiful view of Woodstock and the surrounding hills and mountains can be seen.

Beginning at the clubhouse, ski across the golf course to Brookside trail. Follow Brookside to Evergreen. You will be climbing most of the way, as the route leads up the high ridge visible from the touring center. The trail passes through a stand of hemlock trees and joins the Skinny Dip.

WOODSTOCK-BARNARD

Take a left on Skinny Dip and follow to the junction of the Mt. Peg trail. Take a left here and follow to a spur trail that leads out to the summit of Mt. Peg.

The Mt. Peg trail has a couple of switchbacks on it, which makes the run back easier and safer than if it were a straight shot down. The upper part of the Mt. Peg trail passes through mixed hardwoods (beech and maple) and a stand of red pine. The summit of Mt. Peg is clear, and on a nice day you can see Killington and Mt. Tom to the west, and the hills of Pomfret to the northwest. The large farm below and on the far side of the village is the Billings Farm, now also a museum.

You can ski down the same way you went up or utilize some of the other trails in the system to make a longer run.

For more information contact:
Woodstock Ski Touring Center
Route 106
Woodstock, Vermont 05091

MOUNT TOM

RATING: **Easiest/More Difficult/Most Difficult**
TYPE: **Fee/Groomed**
LENGTH: **24 km**
MAP: **Available at Woodstock Ski Touring Center**
ELEVATION: **700' - 1,250'**

The Mount Tom system of trails is part of the Woodstock Ski Touring Center's complex. Trail tickets can be purchased at the touring center on Route 106.

Most of the trails on Mount Tom are old carriage roads originally built on the estate of Frederick Billings in the 1880's. The first impression you get while skiing in this area is the neat and manicured appearance of the forest. This is due to the fact that it is actively managed by John Wiggin, Director of Ski Touring and Land Use for Laurence S. Rockefeller and for the Woodstock Inn and Resort. This forest is a prime example of intensive woodlot management. Every year some of the timber is selectively logged for various products, with firewood being used in the wood furnaces and fireplaces at the touring center, Suicide Six base lodge and The Woodstock Inn as well as the Rockresort sugar house.

Access to the Mount Tom trails is from two points: next to the cemetery on River St., or from a parking area on Prosper Rd. in West Woodstock. Complete directions appear on the back of the trail map available at the Woodstock Ski Touring Center.

MOUNT TOM - RECOMMENDED TRAIL: SLEIGH RIDE

TYPE: **Groomed**
LENGTH: **7 km (round trip)**
DIFFICULTY: **Easiest**

Sleigh Ride (so named because the trail was, in the past, often used for sleigh rides in winter) begins beyond the Prosper Rd. parking lot. From the road the trail ascends through pine plantations and forks to the right at the junction of the Chutes trail. It then drops through a stand of Norway spruce and at the junction of Spring Lot Trail turns right and passes along the Pogue, a mountain lake once believed to be bottomless. Passing by the lake it ascends through fields, a pine plantation set out in 1887 and, crossing a stone causeway, it passes through old growth hemlocks to the summit of Mount Tom.

At the summit there is a great view of the village of Woodstock 500' below and west to Killington and

WOODSTOCK-BARNARD

east to New Hampshire. Return by following the same route, or explore many of the other trails which branch off from it.

THE SKY LINE TRAIL
RATING: **More Difficult**
TYPE: **Marked and Mapped**
LENGTH: **20 km**
MAP: **USGS Woodstock North/Sky Line Trail map**
ELEVATION: **700' - 1,600'**

The Sky Line Trail is a public trail that was conceived by local conservationist and cross-country ski enthusiast Richard Brett in the early 1940's. Construction was completed in 1963. This trail exists today in most part due to the generosity of the landowners over whose property it passes. As long as skiers are considerate and display good manners while enjoying this popular route, it should remain open to the public.

The trail is now maintained by enthusiastic landowners, interested skiers and the Woodstock Ski Touring Center Staff.

You will note that I have not indicated length of time required to ski this route. Being 20 km long, it is not a trail that most skiers would attempt in its entirety in one day. I have, therefore, broken it up into sections, since this is the way most ski it. The printed map of this trail is available at the Woodstock Ski Touring Center and usually at the Amity Pond shelter. The description of each section is so good on this map that I have used a good part of it here.

HAWK'S HILL TO AMITY POND SHELTER
6 km

The Sky Line Trail begins in the town of Barnard at Hawk's Hill. It leads west from a guest house and after a short distance heads north, crossing a brook and past some small ponds. It now heads east through a pine plantation. The trail goes downhill until it joins the plowed road to Hawk's Hill. Go right on the road and then immediately head southeast down an old roadway. Further on, in a stand of pines, the Pail Trail (an alternate route to the Amity Pond shelter) comes in on the left.

The main route leaves the woods and heads southeast across a field and then descends to the Broad Brook Rd. south of a concrete bridge. From this point to Amity Pond the trail is nearly all uphill.

Across Broad Brook Rd. the trail crosses the brook and enters the Amity Pond Natural Area. The trail now heads south, then turns east, climbing to a junction marked by signs indicating directions to Barnard and Woodstock. At this point you can choose to continue on, or ski to the Amity Pond shelter and entrance. There is parking here along the road for a few cars.

You can also choose to make a loop back to Hawk's Hill by following the Pail Trail.

> WARNING! Remember, it's all downhill on the Pail Trail, so use caution.

From the junction of the Pail Trail, the views off to the west and south are excellent.

AMITY POND TO THE HARVEY FARM
4.8 km

This, combined with the next, are the most heavily skied sections of the trail since it is at a high elevation and offers some of the most scenic views on the route.

If you are starting at this point, there is a shelter

with a register book and maps off the main trail to the southwest a short distance. The main trail climbs to a clear hilltop where it turns south downhill past the Pail Trail. The trail descends through the fields and across two walls, through a swamp and up to a rail fence. Here the trail turns right and passes to the east of a stand of small white pines, and then crosses a field. It angles up through red pines to the Haydock House. Heading south, the trail crosses Skyline Drive. Winding through white pines, you will then pass to the east of a pond and come upon a plowed road. East up the road the trail heads south part way up a steep hill, then heads to the west through hardwoods to the junction of Skyline Drive and Webster Hill Rd.

At this junction there is a choice of two routes. The easiest route crosses Webster Hill Road, enters a field and follows a power line southeast. Following a private wood road it leads to a meadow and turns west to a woodland trail junction. From the junction, the trail heads south to a field and the Harvey Farm.

HARVEY FARM TO SUICIDE SIX
5 km

Crossing the field, the trail climbs to a ridge where there is a magnificent view of the White Mountains to the east. Descending through a maple grove, it enters an abandoned pasture and heads southeast. There is another descent and again a kilometer-plus climb. At this point the trail begins its rapid descent to Suicide Six ski area. Shortly after the descent begins, there is a spur trail to the west which leads to a beautiful vista. It's a short climb worth the extra effort, as there is the summit of Suicide Six below you - quite an ego trip for the skier. If you haven't spotted a car at the ski area, this is the point where you should head back. The rest of the drop to the valley is steep and will require good skiing technique as well as good falling technique. Part way down, near the bottom, the trail turns right behind the Churchill House to ascend a field then by a sugarbush operated by the Woodstock Inn. It finishes its descent through an open slope to Suicide Six, where many spot their car for the shuttle back to the starting point. You might consider lingering for a warm drink in the lodge before heading back.

SUICIDE SIX TO WEST WOODSTOCK PROSPER ROAD
4.7 km

If you choose to continue on to Woodstock, you can follow this trail, which leads to the Mount Tom trail system, which in turn will connect with the village.

This route climbs the ramp to the ski lodge, then heads south across the fields below the smaller chair lift and J-bar lift. The trail continues on the back side of Barnard Brook, and after one kilometer, enters a large field and ascends southwest through a saddle between two hills. It cuts west and descends a steep open slope to Route 12. The trail goes right on Route 12 and in 100 meters leaves the highway, crosses a bridge and continues another 100 meters south on a driveway. It leaves the driveway and heads southwest to a small parking lot on the West Woodstock - Prosper Road.

From here pick a route on the Mount Tom system that will take you to the cemetery entrance on River Road.

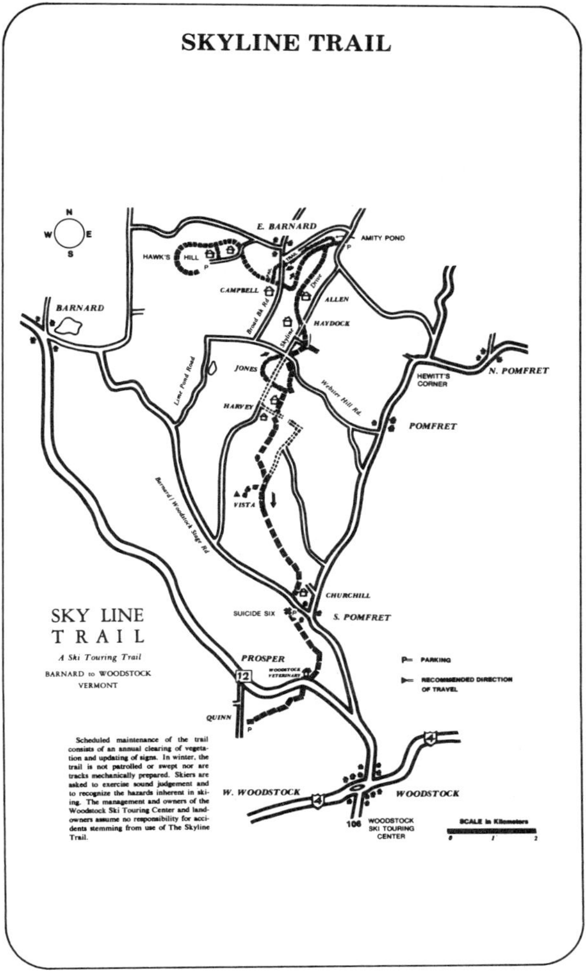

WOODSTOCK-BARNARD 35

SKYLINE TRAIL

SKY LINE TRAIL

A Ski Touring Trail

BARNARD to WOODSTOCK
VERMONT

Scheduled maintenance of the trail consists of an annual clearing of vegetation and updating of signs. In winter, the trail is not patrolled or swept nor are tracks mechanically prepared. Skiers are asked to exercise sound judgement and to recognize the hazards inherent in skiing. The management and owners of the Woodstock Ski Touring Center and landowners assume no responsibility for accidents stemming from use of The Skyline Trail.

QUECHEE LAKES TOURING TRAILS

RATING: **Easiest/More Difficult/Most Difficult**
TYPE: **See description below**
LENGTH: **25 km**
ELEVATION: **500' - 1,000'**

The system of ski touring trails at Quechee Lakes lies within the boundaries of a 3,000 acre green belt, being part of the 6,000 acre Quechee Lakes development. The system is being developed by the property owners' association for use exclusively by property owners, renters (there are over 200 condominiums and 200 homes for rent here), and guests of some of the local inns. At the time of this writing, the trails were not open to the general public. That may change at some point in the future.

The trails pass through mixed hardwoods, some conifer stands, and past beaver ponds. The golf course is also utilized. There are some excellent views of the White River Valley from several vantage points within the system.

All of the trails have been bulldozed, and are groomed in winter.

For further information contact:
  Quechee Club
  P.O. Box 1
  Quechee, Vermont 05059

WILDERNESS TRAILS SKI SCHOOL AND TOURING CENTER

RATING: **Easiest/More Difficult/Most Difficult**
TYPE: **Fee, Groomed**
LENGTH: **40 km**
MAP: **Available at the center**

Situated next to scenic Quechee Gorge, this popular touring center is headquartered at the beautiful Quechee Inn at Marshland Farm. The property was once the farmstead of Colonel Joseph Marsh, Vermont's first Lieutenant Governor.

The center grooms over 10 km of its trail system, has 2 km of lighted trail, instruction, rental equipment, a retail shop, and of course, lodging, and food and beverage are available at the inn.

For further information contact:
 Wilderness Trails Touring Center
 c/o Quechee Inn at Marshland Farm
 Clubhouse Road
 Quechee, Vermont 05059

KEDRON VALLEY INN SKI TOURING CENTER
RATING: **Easiest/More Difficult/Most Difficult**
TYPE: **Fee, Groomed**
MAP: **Available at the center**
LENGTH: **24 km**
ELEVATION: **1,055' - 1,600'**

The trail system at the Kedron Valley Inn passes through open hay fields, and rolling wooded terrain. They follow bridle paths and open logging roads through some very scenic Vermont countryside. The numerous open fields offer wonderful opportunities to carve wide turns when covered with fresh powder snow. A three and a half mile trail connects the Inn to the Woodstock Ski Touring Center.

The center offers instruction, guided tours, rentals, food, lodging, sleigh rides, horseback riding, and ski joring (being pulled through the snow on skis by a horse - not for the meek).

For further information contact:
 Kedron Valley Inn Ski Touring Center
 South Woodstock, Vermont 05071

CHAPTER TWO

Ski The Quechee Inn at Marshland Farm

18km of wooded trails • mid-week ski package

Cross-country learning center • beginners & intermediate trails

Quechee, VT 05059   (802) 295-3133

KEDRON VALLEY INN & MOTEL
SOUTH WOODSTOCK, VERMONT

X-COUNTRY CENTER

Paul & Barbara Kendall, Innkeepers
Open Year Around
Telephone (802) 457-1473

WOODSTOCK-BARNARD 39

The Inn at Mt. Ascutney

Six Quiet, antique furnished, comfortable guest rooms (most with private bath) in this one-time farmhouse - now an intimately charming country inn. Beamed dining room, lounge and open kitchen. Noted for its **country cooking with a continental flair** and carefully selected and balanced wine list. Close to a variety of cross-country skiing experiences. **I-91 to Windsor. West on Rt. 44, 6 mi.** Write "Ann" for free brochure.

802-484-7725
Brownsville, Vt. 05037

Eric & Margaret Rothchild
Innkeepers

the Rumble Seat restaurant

Italian Dishes · Our Specialty

OPEN 12 - 11 PM
WOODSTOCK EAST, WOODSTOCK

WOODSTOCK-BARNARD 41

Woodstock is where you start. From there it's up to you.

It's all here just waiting to be enjoyed. Terrific alpine skiing at the famous Suicide Six ski area. 75 kilometers of cross-country trails at the Woodstock Ski Touring Center. And the wonderful Woodstock Inn to come home to, complete with a 10-foot fireplace—and renowned Rockresorts dining. Plus the picturesque village of Woodstock itself, where you can shop for antiques or stroll across a covered bridge.

Come, get started soon. Special winter sports plans available. See your travel agent, or contact the Inn.

A Rockresort

The Woodstock Inn & Resort
WOODSTOCK • VERMONT • 05091

457-2114   (802) 457-1100   457-1666

The Inn at Weathersfield

An 18th century stagecoach stop nestled at the base of Hawk's Mountain, offering distinctive cuisine in a country setting.

Full bar and extensive wine cellar; live piano nightly.

Spacious bedrooms with operating fireplaces, private baths. Breakfast in bed. Afternoon tea.

Horse-drawn wagon and sleigh rides. Box stalls and paddock facilities. Year-round recreational and cultural facilities nearby.

Featured in *Country Inns and Back Roads,* June '82 *Gourmet Magazine, London Times, Paris Le Monde,* etc. **VISA/M.C.**

Route 106, (Near Perkinsville)
Weathersfield, VT 05151
(802) 263-9217

WOODSTOCK-BARNARD 43

You'll know you're in Vermont!

Valley View Motel

Spectacular views, relaxed atmosphere, reasonable rates.

20 units
AAA approved—
Mobile Travel Guide

802/457-2123

Enes' TABLE

AT VALLEY VIEW

• Ristorante Italiano •
Offering a wide variety of foods from the different regions of Italy. All homemade, prepared fresh daily.

Italian Wines•Cocktails
Dinner 5:30-9:00

Open all year.
Closed Tuesdays.

Mia casa e tua casa.
802/457-2512

Located 5 miles north of Woodstock on Route 12.

You'll swear you're in Italy!

EASTERN COYOTE

The coyote is not a native animal species of Vermont. The first sighting of one in the state was in 1948, and since that time the species has proliferated.

The eastern coyote is believed to have entered Vermont through Canada, and to have attained its greater size (than its western counterpart) by crossbreeding with the timber wolf of Michigan and Ontario.

It is a true scavenger, eating just about anything. Rodents and rabbits are a favorite food, as well as carcases of deer that have died of starvation or been killed by domestic dogs.

The coyote has been ruthlessly persecuted in this country by mankind. Yet the species has accomplished what no other has been able to under the same circumstances - it has actually increased its range. Attempts have been made in New England to establish a bounty on the animal. Fortunately, these attempts have been thwarted thus far.

The eastern coyote is actually a good addition to Vermont's wildlife collection. It is a useful scavenger, cleaning up carrion, and keeping rodent populations under control.

If, while skiing in the backcountry, you are quiet and observant, you just may see a coyote. On a tour in a remote area of southern Vermont in 1983 I encountered one on the trail. Wolf-like in appearance, large bushy tail and thick gray hair, it took one look at me and disappeared back down the trail. Such encounters add a whole new dimension to cross-country ski outings.

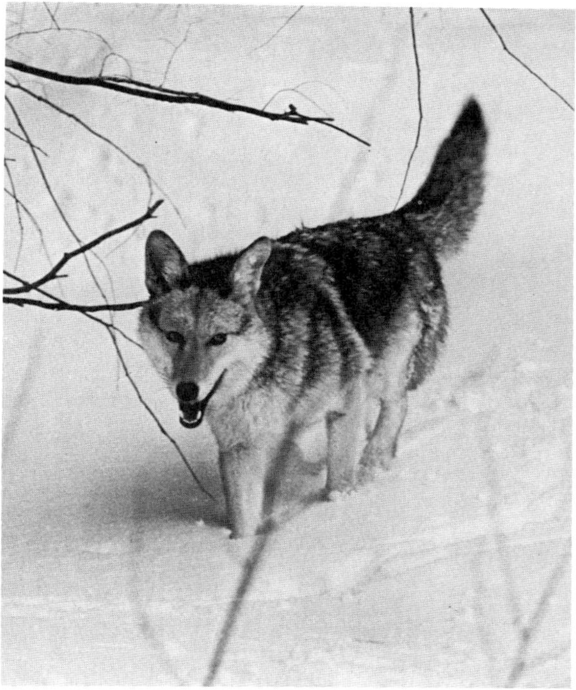

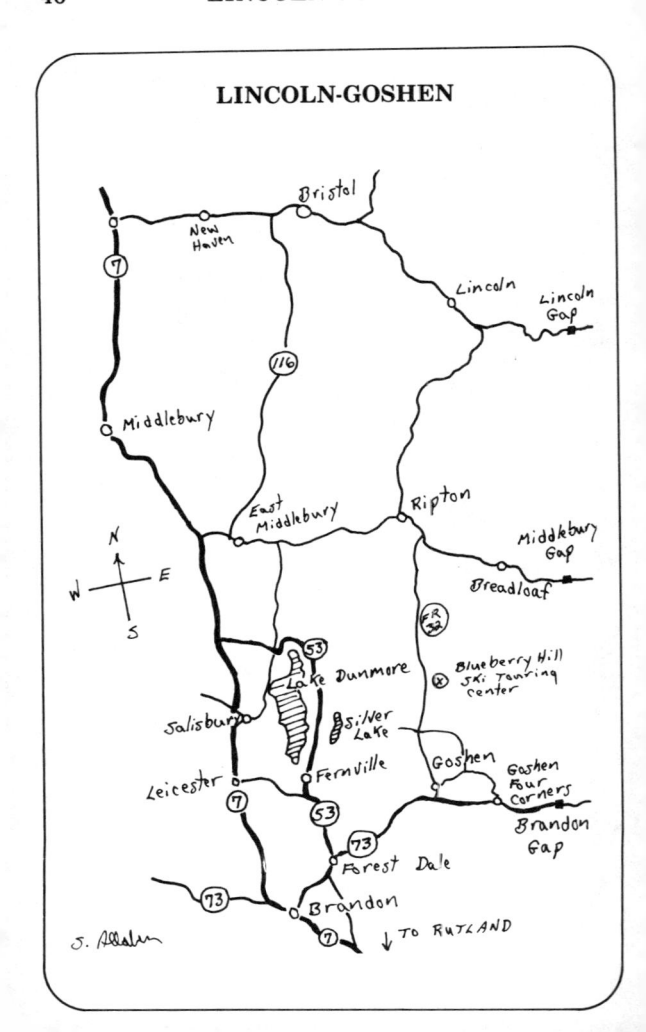

LINCOLN-GOSHEN

CHAPTER THREE

LINCOLN - GOSHEN

The area covered in this chapter is some of the most beautiful and varied within central Vermont. It includes the small mountain towns of Lincoln, Ripton and Goshen, all of which are at high elevations within the Green Mountains and contain a large portion of National Forest land. This was the home of Robert Frost, one of America's most popular poets. When you visit the region you will immediately understand what inspired him to compose so much wonderful poetry.

To the west, in the southern end of the Champlain Valley lie the towns of Middlebury and Brandon. Here you will find a wide variety of lodging facilities, antique and craft shops, and Middlebury College, which has one of the most beautiful campuses that I have ever seen.

The contrast between the topography of the mountain area and the Champlain Valley is strong. It is well worth taking a day off from skiing to explore the vast open farm land to the west of Middlebury. Here is the Dead Creek Waterfowl Area, a state-operated wetland area that is a bird watcher's paradise during all months of the year. It is even skiable when there is snow cover. Dead Creek, with its expanse of marshland and open water offers migrating waterfowl a resting place during spring and autumn.

To fully appreciate the variety of activities and scenic beauty that this area has to offer I highly recommend a visit during the summer or fall.

BLUEBERRY HILL SKI TOURING CENTER

RATING: **Easiest/More Difficult/Most Difficult**
TYPE: **Fee/Groomed**
LENGTH: **60 km**
MAP: **Available at the center**
ELEVATION: **1,500' - 2,500'**

Blueberry Hill is one of Vermont's oldest ski touring centers, and one of its most popular. It is also one of the most written about, as this is where the inn-to-inn cross-country skiing idea began.

Located on the west slope of the Green Mountain Range, Blueberry Hill's trail system offers everything from short mellow loops for the beginner to challenging long runs for the more advanced skier. Having skied the American Ski Marathon here several years ago (Blueberry Hill is the organizer of the annual 60 km race) I can attest to the fact that there are some real challenging downhill runs available here.

The center offers rentals, lessons, a retail ski shop, and a superb country inn with some of the finest food you will find in Vermont. The trail system has several destination tours; the Churchill House, Middlebury Snow Bowl, and Breadloaf Ski Touring Center.

For further information contact:
  Blueberry Hill Ski Touring Center
  Goshen, Vermont 05733

BLUEBERRY HILL S.T.C. - RECOMMENDED TRAIL: HOGBACK

RATING: **More Difficult**
TYPE: **Groomed**
LENGTH: **5 km**
TIME: **1½ - 2 Hours**

LINCOLN-GOSHEN

Although this is not a particularly long tour, it certainly is a pretty one, and well worth doing. It is one of the center's most popular routes, because of the beautiful views along the way.

The trail begins behind the inn where you will see a sign pointing to Hogback. Follow the sign and right away you will cross Dutton Brook, and then pass an open area where the North Goshen schoolhouse and cemetery are located. The trail continues uphill and reaches intersection #9. At this point turn right.

The route now follows the contour of Hogback past some large maple trees over gently rolling terrain. Passing through some open meadows, there is a short, steep hill. You will then pass through a stand of white birch trees, and on into an open clearing where you will find a fantastic view. To the west are the Adirondack mountains, the Taconic ridge to the southwest and the Green Mountains to the east with Brandon Gap at the southwest. In late summer the south end of Hogback is covered with wild blueberries. Areas of the mountain are burned off in the spring to propogate more berries.

The trail now drops down to a road and through a gate. A short distance on you will come to intersection #21, where you will leave the road and get back on a trail starting up the east side of Hogback. There is a scenic ravine to the right with beautiful white and gray birches. The trail goes to the right at intersection #19 through pines, and then left at intersection #23. From here it is all downhill back to the inn.

LONG TRAIL - BRANDON GAP

RATING: **More Difficult**
TYPE: **Wilderness (Hiking trail)**
LENGTH: **8 km (round trip)**
TIME: **3 Hours**
MAP: **Mount Carmel (USFS)**
ELEVATION: **2,180' - 2,950'**

The Long Trail is skiable from Brandon Gap south about 2½ miles. It is a constant uphill climb all the way, although none of it is very steep. The trail is skied a good deal, so you are likely to find tracks here unless you arrive after a fresh snow.

The first section near the road is steep, but only for about 30'. From then on it climbs gently along the contours on the east side of the mountains eventually reaching Sunrise Shelter.

The trail is in the woods all the way. There are some fine views to the east looking through the trees. Before and after the shelter there are two bridges to cross. They are narrow, so use caution.

As you gain elevation you will note the forest growth changes. The trees are smaller and more numerous. Passing through birch and evergreen trees, the trail circles a deep ravine until it reaches the intersection of the Chittenden Brook Trail. At this point you should turn around and ski back as the terrain becomes more rugged and unpleasant to ski.

The Chittenden Brook Trail can be skied down to Chittenden Brook Campground. However, it is steep and narrow and should not be attempted unless you are an excellent backcountry skier.

LINCOLN-GOSHEN

MIDDLE ROAD TRAIL
RATING: **Easiest**
TYPE: **Forest Road**
LENGTH: **7-8 km (round trip)**
TIME: **1-2 Hours**
MAP: **Mount Carmel (USFS)**
ELEVATION: **1,400' - 1,800'**

This road used to be skiable for a far greater distance than it is now, but due to recent home construction at its south end, a good part of the old route is now plowed. So, for the sake of simplicity, I have written the route up as an "out and back" tour.

The trail begins at a point where the Middle Road is no longer plowed near Goshen Four Corners. The trail follows the road ascending gradually through forested land. At 1,700' it levels out more and parallels Basin Brook (to the left). Just before crossing the brook, look to the right. Here there is an old farm road that leads to a clearing where you will find a wonderful view up and down the valley. This is a great spot for a lunch break.

I recommend following the same route back from here, although you can opt to continue on the Middle Road south to the point where plowing begins.

(See map page 14)

CHURCHILL HOUSE SKI TOURING CENTER
RATING: **Easiest/More Difficult/Most Difficult**
TYPE: **Fee/groomed**
LENGTH: **15 km**
MAP: **Available at the center**
ELEVATION: **700' - 1,400'**

The Churchill House is a nineteenth century country inn that also serves as a ski touring center. The 15 km trail system utilizes logging roads in the nearby Green Mountain National Forest. It is also connected by trail to Blueberry Hill Ski Touring Center, and is actively involved with inn-to-inn skiing with three other inns.

More trails are planned for future years, so expect the skiing opportunities to increase here each year. One of the most popular trails is the route from the inn to Silver Lake. This is an easy trail that runs along a beautiful brook to its destination.

For further information write:
The Churchill House Inn
Route 73
Brandon, Vermont 05733

NORSKE TRAIL

RATING: **More Difficult**
TYPE: **Marked/Primitive**
LENGTH: **8 km (round trip)**
MAP: **Breadloaf (USFS)**
ELEVATION: **1,600' - 1,900'**

The Norske Trail connects the Middlebury Snow Bowl Ski Area to the Breadloaf Campus of Middlebury College (Breadloaf Ski Touring Center). It is marked with blue diamonds and is maintained by local skiers.

The entrance to the trail is just west of the Snow Bowl entrance on the north side of route 125. The trail heads north west following a logging road. There are several large water bars to cross at the beginning and then the trail enters a cleared area at the top of a hill. From here it drops gradually to a stream crossing and through an old log landing on the other side of the stream.

It crosses a second stream dropping gradually to another small tributary. Crossing the third bridge, the trail climbs gradually following an old skid road.

LINCOLN-GOSHEN

Entering deep hardwoods it winds around the shoulder of a hill (from here there is a view down to the Breadloaf Campus) and continues on over level terrain through mixed forest. There is then a sharp, steep drop around a corner to a bridge. Caution! This approach is tricky. Following a gentle downhill through fir trees the trail crosses the Burnt Hill Trail (a hiking trail). At this point you have the option to ski down the trail to Forest Road 59 or to continue on to the right on the main trail.

If you continue on, the trail passes through hardwoods onto a new logging road. There is a good fast downhill run to Forrest Road 59. At the road, go right 100 yards. The trail goes to the left into mixed hardwoods descending into a red pine plantation and eventually comes out at the Gilmore House at the Breadloaf Campus. At this point you will be entering the Breadloaf Ski Touring Center trail system, which is a fee system. Return by the same route.

NATURAL TURNPIKE

RATING: **Easiest**
TYPE: **Forest Service Road**
LENGTH: **12 km**
MAP: **Lincoln and Breadloaf (USFS)**
ELEVATION: **1,750' - 2,000'**

The Natural Turnpike is a wide Forest Service road that is normally not plowed in the winter unless there is a logging project underway. You may wish to contact the Forest Service office in Middlebury to get an up-to-date report on its status. It also serves as a snowmobile trail, so expect to encounter snowmobilers on occasion. The road serves as one of the routes used by skiers to travel inn-to-inn from the Long Run Inn in Lincoln to the Chipman Inn in Ripton.

The route passes through mixed hardwood and conifer forest, some of which has been recently logged. There are also some open meadows, brooks and beaver ponds close by.

The Natural Turnpike is accessible from both the North and South ends. Part of it is plowed on a regular basis on the north end, and at the south can be reached from Forest Road 59 (see map). There is limited parking at both ends. The total distance between the two ends is 12 km.

ROBERT FROST FARM

RATING: **Easiest**
TYPE: **Fields, woods road**
LENGTH: **4 km**
MAP: **East Middlebury (USFS)**
ELEVATION: **1,500'**

The Robert Frost Farm is a national registered historic landmark, and is situated in a high mountain plateau, surrounded by fields and forest land. There are some beautiful views from many points around the farm house. Although there are no trails to speak of (except for the Fire Tower Hill trail at the Breadloaf Ski Touring Center that connects the two locations) the old homestead is a wonderful place to poke around on skis, and to sit and read some of Frost's poetry while enjoying the beauty that surrounds you.

There is a woods road to the right of the house that leads into a red pine plantation. It follows a gentle uphill course for a short distance. Beyond this is one of the Breadloaf touring center's trails, which should be approached from the center, not the Frost farm.

The road leading into the farm is now plowed in winter, and at the end is parking for a half dozen cars.

LINCOLN-GOSHEN

BREADLOAF SKI TOURING CENTER
RATING: **Easiest/More Difficult/Most Difficult**
TYPE: **Fee/Groomed**
LENGTH: **35 km**
MAP: **Available at the center**
ELEVATION: **1,400' - 1,800'**

The site of the start of the American Ski Marathon in past years, Breadloaf is situated on Route 125 in the village of Ripton. The trail system passes through open meadows, hardwood and conifer forests over rolling terrain in the heart of the Green Mountains.

The Firetower Hill trail passes by the Robert Frost Farm, a national historic site. Operated by Middlebury College, the center offers instruction and rentals.

For further information contact:
Breadloaf Ski Touring Center
Ripton, Vermot 05766

CHAPTER THREE

ROBERT FROST FARM
BREADLOAF SKI TOURING CENTER

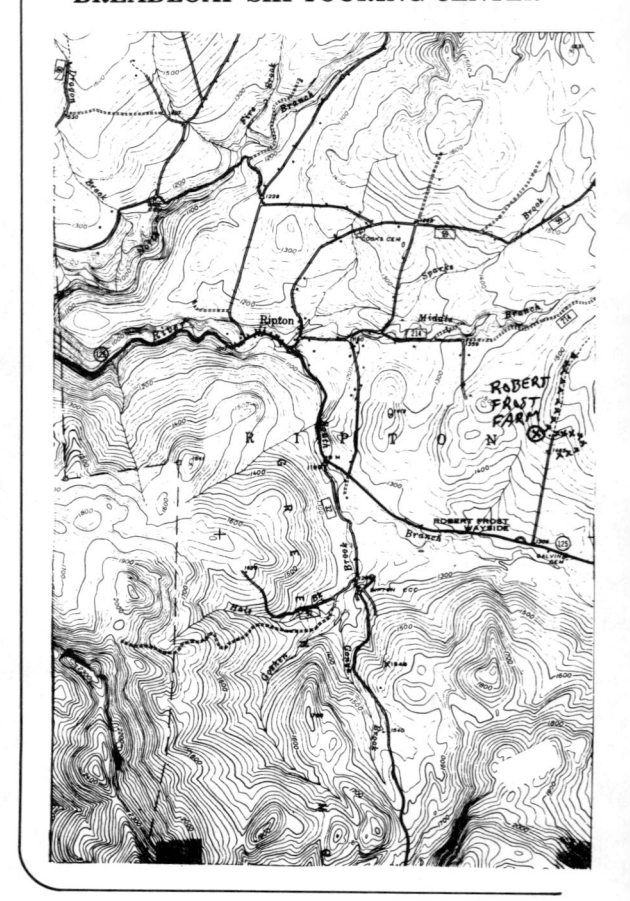

LINCOLN-GOSHEN

NATURAL TURNPIKE
FOREST ROAD 59
NORSKE TRAIL

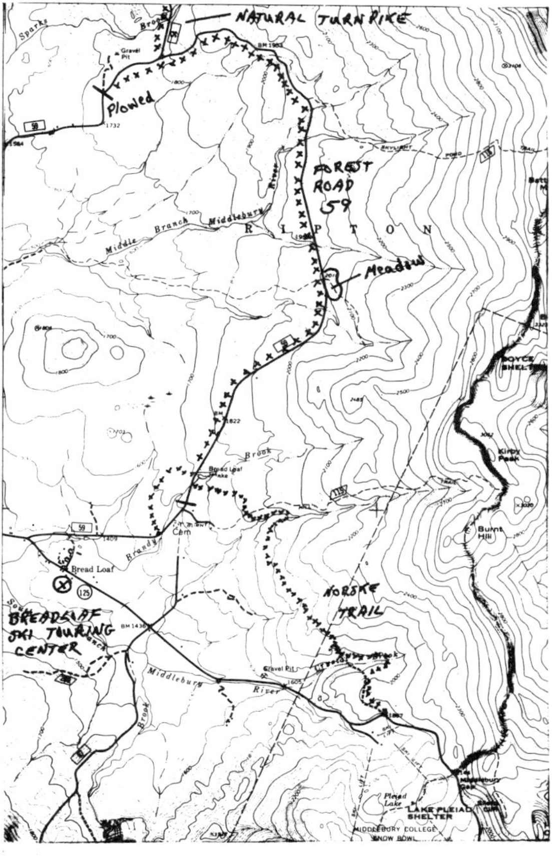

CHAPTER THREE

FOREST ROAD 59

RATING: **Easiest**
TYPE: **USFS Road**
LENGTH: **14 km**
MAP: **Breadloaf (USFS)**
ELEVATION: **1,600' - 2,000'**

Normally not plowed in winter, this Forest Service road is wide and easy to ski. It also serves as a snowmobile trail. The gain in elevation from one end to the other is gentle, and there are no difficult sections. There are many fine views along the way, and several narrower logging roads that diverge left and right that can be explored.

At one point the road passes the beginning of the Skylight Pond Trail, which is a steep hiking trail that climbs east to the top of Battell Mountain and Skylight Pond. Where this trail joins the road there is a large open meadow - a fine spot for a winter picnic. Near the north end, the road converges with Forest Road 54 (the Natural Turnpike).

The best way to ski this route is to leave a car at either end, and start from the south. The road can be found by following Route 125 past the Robert Frost Wayside, and take the first left (north) road. This is FR 59, and is plowed for about one mile. Park off the road here and begin to ski.

The north end is actually called Steammill Road and is reached from the village of Ripton (see map).

BEAVER MEADOWS TRAIL

RATING: **Easiest**
TYPE: **Logging road**
LENGTH: **5 km (round trip)**
MAP: **South Mountain (USFS)**
ELEVATION: **1,440' - 1,600'**

Because this trail follows rather flat terrain, and is not clearly distinguishable all the way to the meadows, one should be sure to bring a compass to avoid getting lost.

The trail is reached by driving up the Notch Road from Route 116 northeast of Middlebury. There are apple orchards near the beginning of the trail. It follows an old logging road south through mixed hardwoods most of the way to the meadows. When the road disappears you should take a compass bearing slightly west of south and follow it until you come to the beaver ponds. Follow the same route back to your car.

DRAGON BROOK TRAIL

RATING: **Easiest**
TYPE: **Logging Road**
LENGTH: **8 km (Round trip)**
MAP: **East Middlebury and South Mountain (USFS)**
ELEVATION: **1,600' - 1,900'**

This trail follows a logging road to Abbey Pond, a small, high elevation body of water east of Middlebury. The trail has very little elevation change, so is a good route for less experienced skiers to venture off on.

It can be reached by driving east on Route 125 from Middlebury, and just before the highway crosses the Middlebury River turn left onto Forest Road 90. Usually plowed in winter, this road leads uphill to a house at the end of the plowed section. Here there is very limited parking, and the trail starts.

The logging road is clearly defined at least half way to Abbey Pond, and then it gets narrower. It leads all the way to the pond, and once there the way back is the same as you followed going in.

CHAPTER THREE

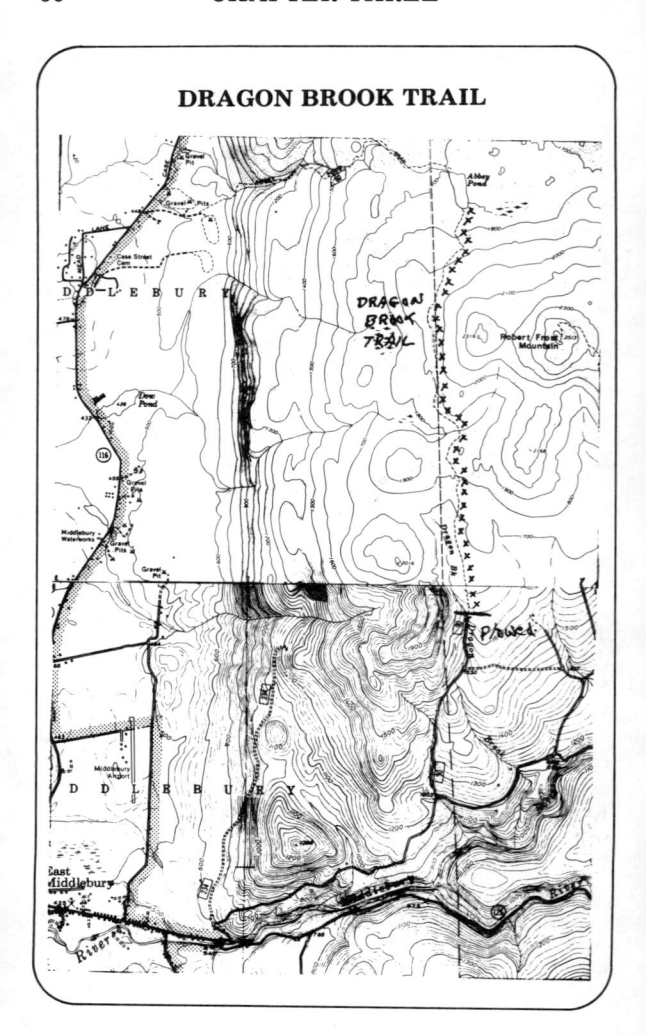

DRAGON BROOK TRAIL

WILD TURKEY

Once a native bird to much of Vermont, the wild turkey disappeared from the state in the mid 1800's due to eradication of its habitat as a result of timber harvesting, and a severe blight that virtually destroyed all the chestnut trees (a major food source for the bird).

When the forests began to grow back in Vermont, oak trees spread throughout a good deal of the state, providing a new food source for the birds, as well as improved habitat.

Because turkeys do not migrate, the Vermont Fish and Game Department imported thirty-one wild birds from Pennsylvania in 1969 in an effort to reintroduce the species. The birds were released in the southwestern corner of the state. The results far surpassed anybody's dreams of success. The turkey now inhabits most areas of the state where there is suitable habitat.

Turkeys spend most of their time foraging for food on the ground. They don't do much flying, although when they have to, they can fly up over high trees and soar on wings (with a spread of up to sixty inches) as far as a mile. In the evenings they roost in trees.

CHAPTER THREE

"Inn-comparable"

Churchill House Inn · R.D. 3
Brandon, Vermont 05733

(802) 247-3300

LINCOLN-GOSHEN 63

X-COUNTRY SKIERS

Once upon a time there was a little ski shop nestled in the heart of Middlebury called Skihaus. Through hard work & a lot of care the little ski shop grew & grew. Today Skihaus still carries skis, but they've added so much more. Come in & get to know us!

Skihaus

in the ✈ of Middlebury, Vt.

THE CHIPMAN INN
RIPTON VERMONT

THE BULLOCK FAMILY   05766
Innkeepers   (802) 388-2390

CHAPTER THREE

LINCOLN-GOSHEN 65

Waybury Inn
Since 1810

Route 125
East Middlebury,
Vermont 05740

One thing leads to another at the
Waybury Inn

Comfortable Lodging

and another...

Fireside Dining

and another...

**Live Entertainment in the Pub
Friday & Saturday nights**

and another...

**A Registered Historic Place
individually decorated and
stenciled rooms**

*Everyone's Gathering Place
For 173 Years*

*Food • Spirits
• Lodging*

The Historic Brandon Inn

Brandon, VT 05733

Established 1786

In the heart of Central Vermont's nordic and alpine skiing. Ski Blueberry Hill, Churchill House, High Pond and Breadloaf for nordic; Killington, Pico, Middlebury Snowbowl for alpine. Then back to this historic country inn, the warmth of a fireplace mingling with happy people. Antique and old-fashioned furnishings, exceptionally fine candle-lite dining, great wines. Inn operated in friendly, caring way of an era gone by. Memorable.

Early reservations please. For considerate skiers. Ask about 3 & 5-Day Packages.

**Call 802/247-5766
Or Write: Innkeeper, Box SA84**

LINCOLN-GOSHEN 67

Long Run Lodge
1799

Enjoy country life in a cozy homelike atmosphere.

Break trail and discover the scenic back roads of the mountain village of Lincoln.

Shuttle available to Sugarbush and Mad River Glen areas.

Innkeepers: Mike & Bev Conway
(802) 453-3233

Write: RD 1, Box 114
Bristol, Vermont 05443

68　　　　　　　　CHAPTER THREE

make tracks to _ _ _ _

THE POHLE FAMILY
WELCOMES YOU

Brandon Motor Lodge
(2 MILES SOUTH OF TOWN)

U.S. RTE. 7 - R.D. #1
BRANDON, VERMONT 05733　　　802-247-9594

CHAPTER FOUR

ROCHESTER - HANCOCK

The area in this chapter includes the towns of Stockbridge and Pittsfield as well as Rochester and Hancock. It is not a highly developed area, being mostly forest land and farms. The White River has its origin not far to the north and flows through a wide valley southward to the Connecticut River.

The terrain to either side of the White River Valley is rugged, however, this does not preclude it as unsuitable for cross-country skiing. On the contrary, there are some fine skiing opportunities in and around the surrounding mountains both to the east and west. This will become obvious as you read through the following trail descriptions.

A great deal of the land in this area is part of the Green Mountain National Forest and therefore, open to skiing. Historically there has not been a great deal of cross-country skiing activity here, so you will not find much in the way of mapped and marked trails.

In the spring the White and Tweed Rivers offer some of the finest white water canoeing and kyaking opportunities in Vermont. If you are one who participates in either activity, you can have a real mixed bag of outdoor sports by skiing the high country (where snows hang on into late April) one day, and hitting the white water another.

CHAPTER FOUR

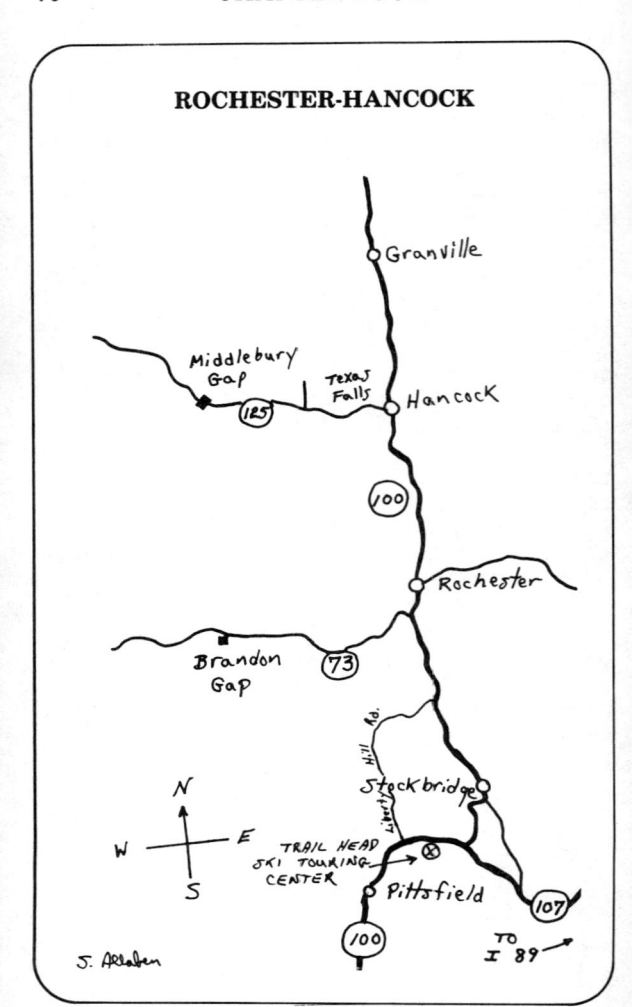

HANCOCK BRANCH BROOK TRAIL

RATING: **Easiest**
TYPE: **Forest Road**
LENGTH: **5 km**
TIME: **2-3 Hours**
MAP: **Breadloaf (USFS)**
ELEVATION: **1,300' - 1,700'**

This route begins just beyond the gate at Forest Road 39 (see Texas Gap Trail), being a spur road that heads to the northwest along Hancock Branch Brook. On the map it is marked as Forest Road 212.

The trail begins on flat terrain, immediately crossing Texas Brook over a wooden bridge. It then climbs gently through a narrow valley along the brook. At the second bridge there is a nice view straight ahead of Burnt Hill in the distance.

After the third bridge the trail climbs quickly and then levels out, coming to a fourth bridge. This bridge is tricky to cross as the bank is washed out at the far end. The trail then enters a recently logged area and passes through an open log landing. It then crosses the fifth bridge and passes through another log landing. At this point the road ends. Follow the same route back.

TEXAS GAP TRAIL

RATING: **Easiest/More Difficult**
TYPE: **Forest Road**
LENGTH: **10 km (round trip to Texas Gap)**
TIME: **3-4 Hours**
MAP: **Breadloaf (USFS)**
ELEVATION: **1,300' - 2,200'**

To get to the beginning of this trail take Forest Road 39 from Route 125 west of the town of Hancock. The road is plowed to a parking area about 1 mile from Route 125. At this point the road is blocked by a gate. This is the beginning of the route. Be aware that this route is also used by snowmobiles.

The road proceeds gently uphill along Texas Brook and very soon will meet Forest Road 212 to the left. Stay on the main road, which continues climbing through a mixture of hardwoods and hemlock. The road crosses the brook and now is not as steep as the first section. After about 1½ km another forest road enters on the left. This is a dead end road and is not worth exploring. A similar road will be encountered a short distance beyond this point.

At the 3 km point the road flattens out and passes through some large open meadows on either side. From this area there are some great views of the surrounding mountains. Another dead end forest road veers off to the right.

The road is now very straight and nearly flat. At the 3½ km point the road forms a Y. The right branch is a fairly new logging road. The main route proceeds straight ahead. The road is now narrower and continues on relatively level terrain for a short distance, then begins a steep uphill climb to Texas Gap. At the top of the gap you can turn around and begin the exhilarating downhill run back, or opt to continue on following the road to the junction of Forest Road 55, which leads east to the town of Granville.

The last section of the route to Texas Gap is not recommended for beginners, because of the steep descent coming back. If you go all the way through to Granville, you will need to leave a vehicle at either end. The entire trip is about 10-12 km.

BINGO BROOK TRAIL

RATING: **Easiest**
TYPE: **Forest Road**
LENGTH: **10 km (round trip)**
TIME: **3-4 Hours**
MAP: **Breadloaf (USFS)**
ELEVATION: **1,300' - 1,800'**

This route is actually Forest Road 42, which connects to Route 73 at a sharp turn in the highway. You can drive in 2-3 miles to a point where the road is no longer plowed. Begin skiing following the road straight ahead on level terrain. After about 2 km of skiing the road is intersected by another road (FR 62) on the right.

The trail passes through open hardwoods and a spruce stand (log landing here) and climbs gently to a point where it dead ends at the foot of a steep ravine. It's easy going all the way and the return trip is all gently downhill. Although not a particularly interesting route it is a pleasant ski for beginners.

CHAPTER FOUR

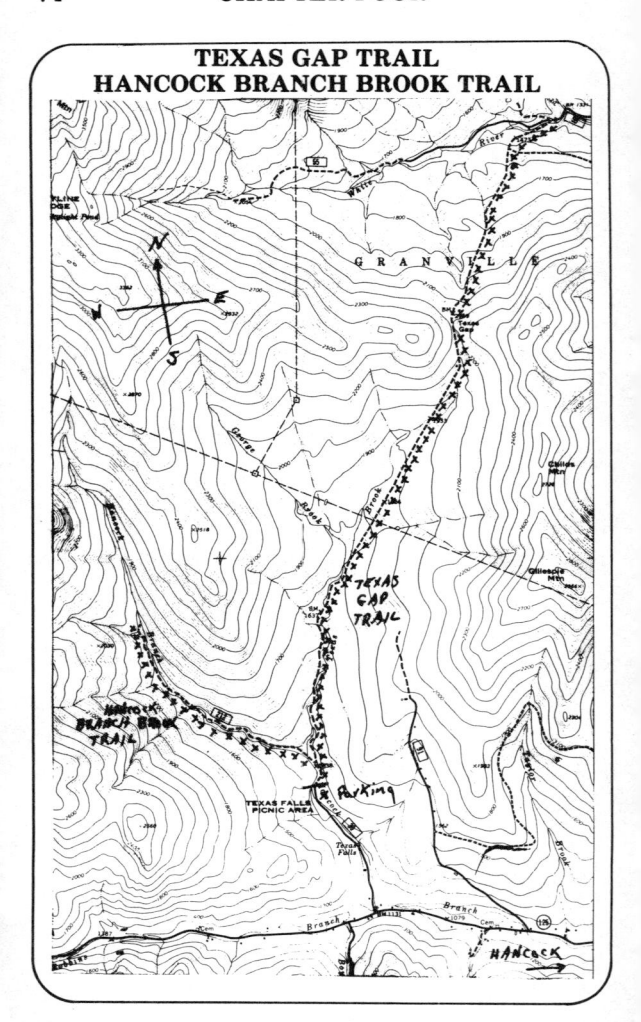

TEXAS GAP TRAIL
HANCOCK BRANCH BROOK TRAIL

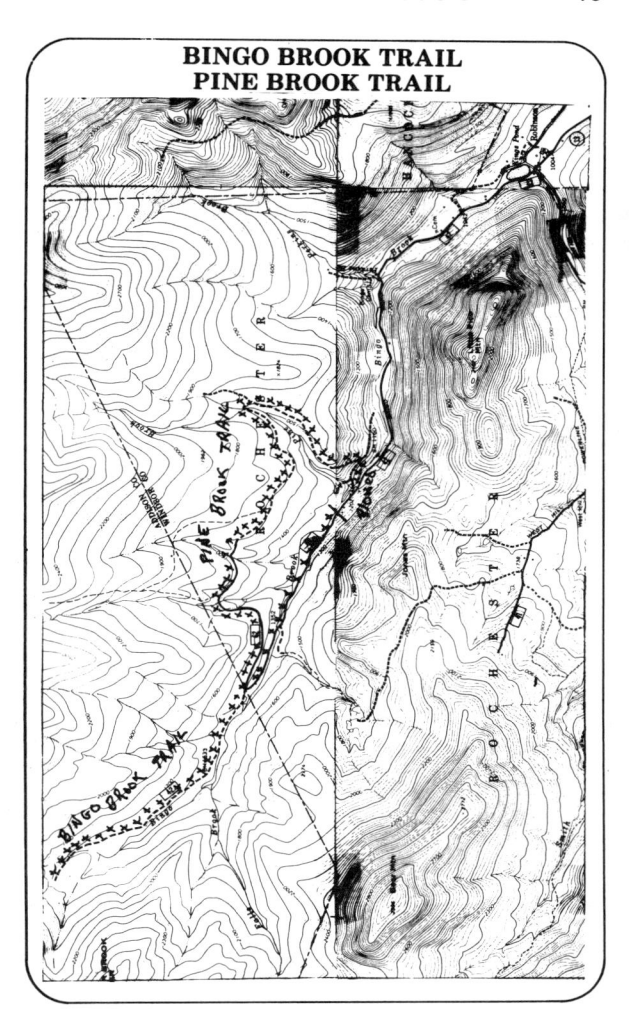

ROCHESTER-HANCOCK

BINGO BROOK TRAIL
PINE BROOK TRAIL

PINE BROOK TRAIL

RATING: **Easiest/More Difficult**
TYPE: **Forest Road**
LENGTH: **7-8 km**
TIME: **3-4 Hours**
MAP: **Mount Carmel/Breadloaf (USFS)**
ELEVATION: **1,200' - 1,600'**

This trail is actually Forest Road 62 which forms a loop off of Forest Road 42. It is one of the nicest tours I found in the Rochester area with pleasant terrain and some gorgeous views.

The trail begins at a point about 2½ miles from Route 73 off of FR 42. Just before a red house on the left there is a bridge to the right that crosses Bingo Brook. This is the beginning of the tour. Ski across the bridge and up a hill. Bear right on the road (the left fork leads to a private cottage) and follow it to a point where a road diverges sharply to the left with a gate. Take this left.

The road climbs steeply uphill through a large stand of hemlock trees. Pine Brook is far below in a ravine. Coming out of the hemlocks, the trail climbs more gently through open hardwoods and eventually crosses Pine Brook (there is no longer a bridge here). At this point you will enter a large log landing and from here on the road is much wider.

The trail follows level terrain mixed with downhill sections as it descends back to FR 42. The rest of the route passes through several different logged over areas where there are some excellent views to the southwest.

Once you come down to the intersection of FR 42, take a left and follow this road back to the starting point.

(See Warning Next Page)

ROCHESTER-HANCOCK

> WARNING! This route should only be skied counter-clockwise, as to do otherwise would entail an extremely difficult downhill run at the end.

LIBERTY HILL
RATING: **Easiest/More Difficult**
TYPE: **Forest Roads**
LENGTH: **15 km**
MAP: **Rochester (USFS)**
ELEVATION: **1,000' - 1,700'**

The Liberty Hill area lies to the west of Route 100 between Rochester and Stockbridge. It is accessible from several points, with very limited parking at each. The area encompasses several old roads that interconnect each other. Off of the main roads are other, more primitive, roads that can be explored.

Rather than give a description of each road and to recommend specific routes, I will leave it to the reader to decide where he or she wishes to ski. In general, the area is interspersed with large open meadows, offering magnificent views up and down the White River Valley. At the triangle formed by the junction of Forest Road 223 (Liberty Hill Rd.) and Forest Road 228 there is a pretty open meadow that offers a spectacular view of Killington and Pico Peaks far to the south.

This area offers some of the finest cross-country skiing in the Rochester area. None of it is particularly difficult, unless you choose to explore one of the side trails that climb to higher elevations.

At the north end the best place to park is on Liberty Hill Rd. at the point where the plowing ends. From Route 100 turn west, north of the White River Golf Course. The road gets very steep, so be sure you are driving a suitable vehicle. There is no parking available on Forest Road 227, which runs to the north off of Liberty Hill Road.

At the south end, access can be attained from two points. Turn north off of Route 100 about one mile east of Pittsfield onto Liberty Hill Road (no road sign here). At the brook crossing another road branches to the left (FR 228) and the main road continues straight ahead. You can take either road and park where the plowing ends.

TRAIL HEAD SKI TOURING CENTER
RATING: **Easiest/More Difficult/Most Difficult**
TYPE: **Fee/Groomed**
MAP: **Available at the center**
ELEVATION: **800' - 1,800'**

Trail Head Ski Touring Center is located on Route 100 along the Tweed River south of Rochester. The 45 km trail system includes everything from very flat, open fields, to more difficult wooded mountain sides.

The center offers rentals, instruction, guided tours, a retail shop and groomed trails. There is even a suspension bridge across the Tweed River giving access to more skiable terrain on the east side.

For further information write:
   Trail Head Ski Touring Center
   Route 100
   Stockbridge, Vermont 05772

ROCHESTER-HANCOCK 79

**TRAIL HEAD SKI TOURING CENTER
LIBERTY HILL TRAILS**

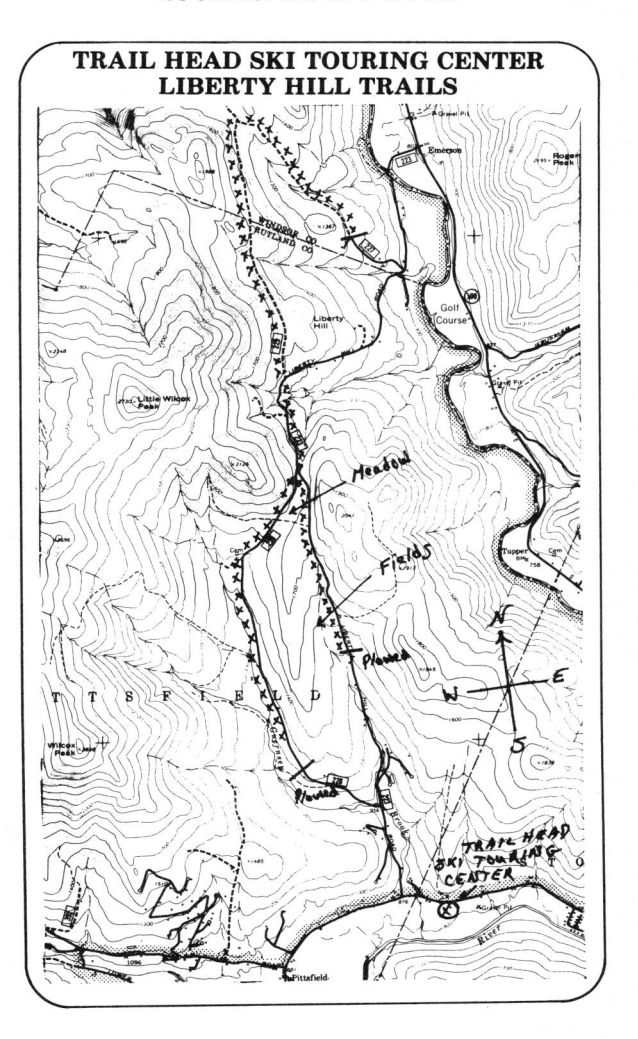

CHITTENDEN BROOK TRAIL
RATING: **More Difficult/Most Difficult**
TYPE: **Forest Road/Trail**
LENGTH: **10-12 km**
TIME: **3-4 Hours**
MAP: **Mount Carmel (USFS)**
ELEVATION: **1,200' - 1,900'**

This trail incorporates a wide road that leads to a Forest Service operated campground, and a narrow ski trail constructed by the Youth Conservation Corps. under the direction of the Forest Service. When I skied it one of the bridges was out and the trail section was not well marked or maintained. You should check with the Forest Service at the Rochester office to determine the status of the trail.

The trail begins from a parking area along Route 73 west of Rochester. There is a large sign here, so it is easy to find. Follow the wide road, which parallels Joe Smith Brook. The going is easy at the start and you will soon cross two bridges. At a point just before a steep hill the trail diverges to the right (this is the beginning of the section cut by the YCC). You can choose at this point to follow the entire route, or to stick to the main road and ski up and back the same way. If you do the entire loop, ski it counterclockwise. To do otherwise would be pure folly, as it is a treacherous route skied clockwise.

Leaving the road the trail climbs gently along a brook and farther on passes close to a cliff (left) where there will be a large ice formation. It then climbs more steeply and crosses a footbridge. The climbing continues at varying degrees and then levels out somewhat, turning left and crossing a small brook (no bridge).

After more climbing the trail levels out again and

then turns abruptly left dropping quickly to a footbridge.

> CAUTION! This is an unsafe approach to the bridge. Above the bridge are some beaver ponds. It would actually be safer to cross the ponds and then get back to the trail.

The trail again climbs until you reach a junction where you can choose an expert route (left) or an intermediate route (right). Don't even think about taking the expert route - it's horrible. The trail gets very narrow through here and eventually comes out into an open area where severe winds (over 100 miles per hour) blew down all the trees in a very large area.

The trail now begins its descent to the campgrounds. There is one more bridge to cross (another dangerous approach) and then the trail joins a logging road which drops rapidly to the campground. From this point on, the road is wide allowing plenty of room for turning (or falling). There is one steep downhill as you approach the point where the loop began, and then you re-trace your tracks to the parking area.

There are some good views from an area just below the campground.

CHAPTER FOUR

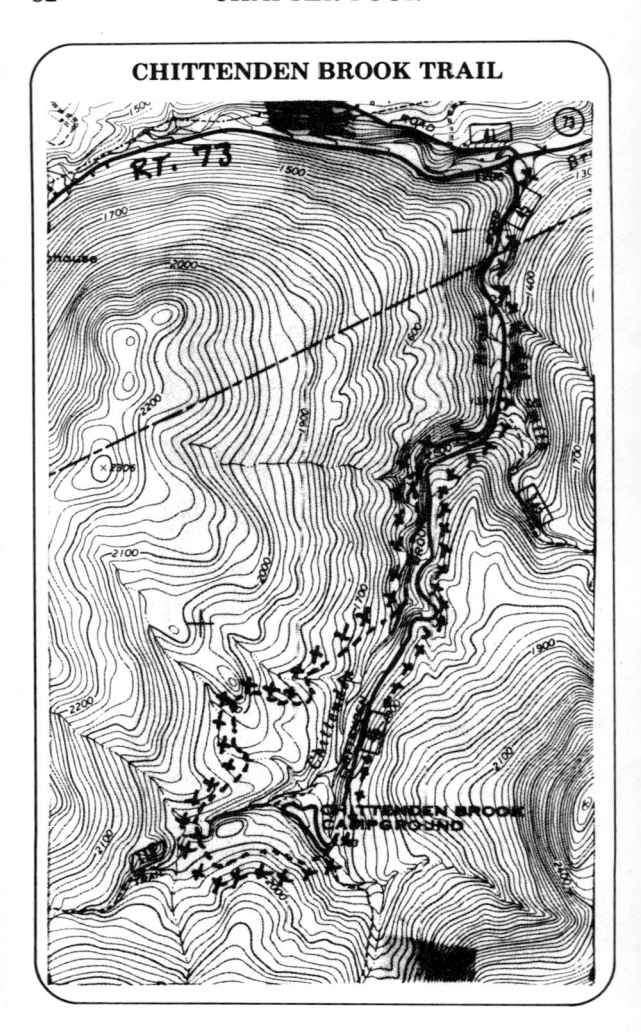

CHITTENDEN BROOK TRAIL

NORTH POND TRAIL

RATING: **Most Difficult**
TYPE: **Forest Road and Trail**
LENGTH: **12 km (round trip)**
TIME: **4-5 Hours**
MAP: **Rochester/Mount Carmel/Chittenden (USFS)**
ELEVATION: **1,000' - 2,500'**

This is definitely a route for experts only. The trail is very steep and narrow in several places, and since it is not maintained at all, may have down trees across it along the way.

The first section is fairly easy following the Townsend Brook Trail (see page 84). When you get to the Old Stage Road, turn left. The trail begins a long steep climb going from 1,600' to 2,100' in less than 2 km. It crosses a couple of brooks in a northwesterly direction, and then turns west following the contour and then climbing again. Townsend Brook is off to the left and below the trail.

After more steep climbing the trail reaches North Pond. On the opposite side of the pond is a steep cliff. Because of the topography around the pond, there is an incredible echo when you make any loud noise.

The Long Trail crosses the ridge to the west, and if you can get up on it you may be able to get a view out across Chittenden Reservoir 1,000' below.

Follow the same route back using extreme caution on the downhill sections.

WARNING! Do not attempt this tour unless you are a very strong skier.

TOWNSEND BROOK TRAIL

RATING: **Easiest/More Difficult**
TYPE: **Forest Road**
LENGTH: **7-8 km**
TIME: **2½-3½ Hours**
MAP: **Rochester (USFS)**
ELEVATION: **1,000' - 1,500'**

To get to the trail head on Townsend Brook Road turn off of Route 100 about 1¾ mile south of the center of Pittsfield. The turnoff is on the west side of Route 100. Follow this road straight past Tozier Hill Road, crossing Townsend Brook to a point where the plowing ceases.

The trail follows the road, with the brook to the right, through hardwood forest. The terrain is fairly level mixed with gentle uphill. At a point where two brooks converge there is a trail off to the right that climbs up to another road known as the Old Stage Road.

At the intersection of the trail and the road, turn right and follow the road, which descends gradually to a point where it is plowed. This is the end of Tozier Hill Road, which you will have to walk down about 1¾ miles to the starting point.

GRANVILLE GULF TRAIL

RATING: **Easiest/More Difficult**
TYPE: **Forest Road**
LENGTH: **8-10 km**
MAP: **Warren and Hancock (USFS)**
ELEVATION: **1,400' - 1,500'**

Along Route 100 between Granville and Warren is a six mile stretch of land on either side of the road that is a state reservation established to protect the natural beauty of the area. Just below Granville

Notch in a flat section is a road that heads south off of Route 100. This is the trailhead, and next to it is a large parking area. This trail is also known as the Puddledock Trail.

The trail follows the old road through mixed forest. It climbs gradually for awhile, and then levels off. About 2½ km in, an old road branches off to the east, climbing up to an old apple orchard. This is a nice site for a picnic. Opposite the road to the west is a long series of beaver ponds.

You can ski the road south to the intersection of the Kendall Brook Road, at which point you may find it plowed. There are several old woods roads off of the main trail that can be explored. Return to the starting point by following the same route.

CARYL BROOK TO MICHIGAN BROOK TRAIL
RATING: **More Difficult**
TYPE: **Forest Road**
LENGTH: **15 km**
TIME: **4-5 Hours**
MAP: **Rochester and Mount Carmel (USFS)**
ELEVATION: **1,000' - 2,200'**

Being such a long loop, this route should only be skied by strong experienced skiers. To get to the trailhead take the Lower Michigan Road just below the center of Pittsfield and follow it to Cero's Furniture Barn.

The trail follows the unplowed road along the West Branch of the Tweed River. The skiing is very easy along gentle terrain until it reaches the third brook crossing. It then climbs more steeply along Caryl Brook (on the left - south), crossing the brook twice before dead ending. At this point you must bushwack by following a compass bearing almost due west until you hit a Forest Service road. To the west of the road a short distance is Beaver Meadows, a series of beaver ponds.

From this point follow the road north. The road follows the contours climbing gradually and then dropping from the 2,200' elevation until it reaches the Wetmore Gap Trail. The road now heads east continuing its descent to the Michigan Road. Go right on the Michigan Road and follow it downhill to a point where it is plowed.

From this point you will have to walk down the road about a mile until you come to an unplowed road on the right that connects back to Lower Michigan Road just below the trailhead.

ROCHESTER-HANCOCK 87

TOWNSEND BROOK TRAIL
NORTH POND TRAIL

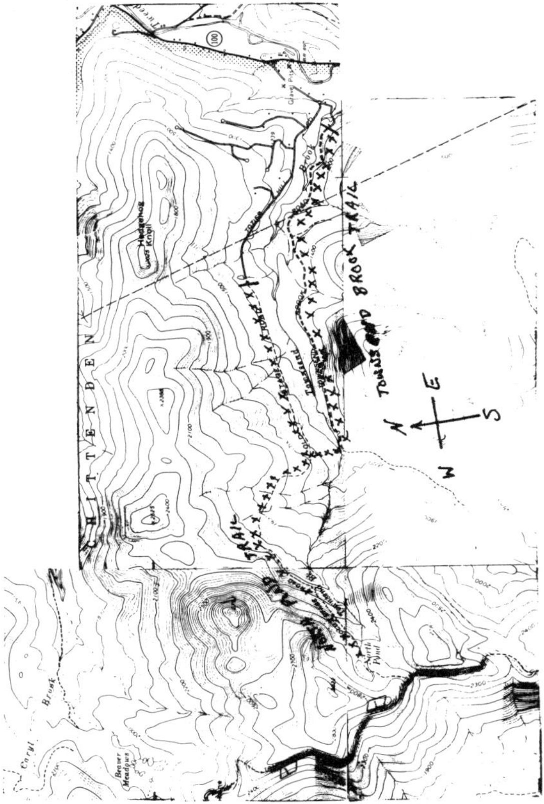

CARYL BROOK TO MICHIGAN BROOK TRAIL

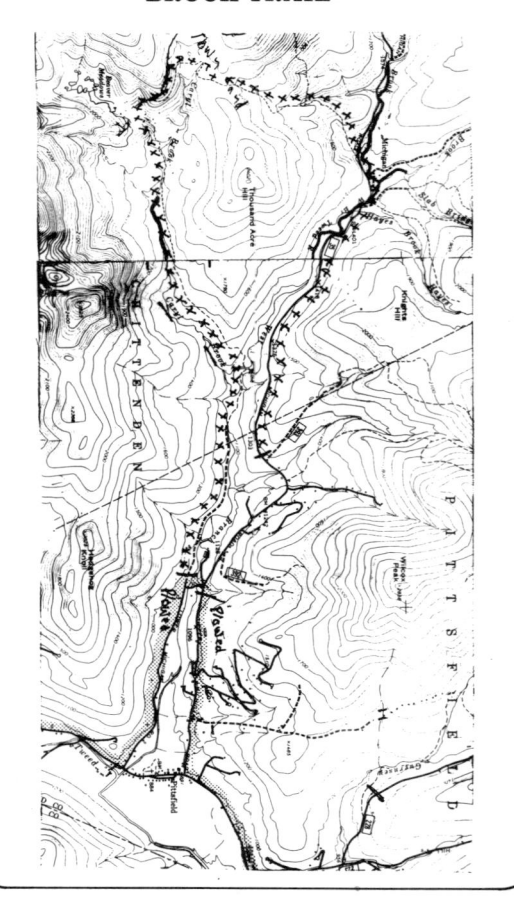

ROCHESTER-HANCOCK 89

Pittsfield Inn

A fine old Inn that caters to outdoor enthusiasts.

Superb continental cuisine & antique furnishings throughout.

Box 526
Pittsfield, Vt. 05762
(802) 746-8943

Huntington House

An Inn & Restaurant

**On the Green
Route 100, Rochester, VT
802/767-3511**

*Located in the Heart of the Green Mountains.
Central to Killington or Sugarbush X-C Ski
Centers. Guided Tours Available.*

EASTERN SNOW SNAKE

Of the various wildlife species that inhabit central Vermont, there is only one that poses any degree of threat to the unsuspecting skier. I don't think it has actually ever been seen, let alone photographed. Yet to those of us who have taken headers into a snow drift, or landed on any icy slope butt end first, we know for a fact that it inhabits the country over which our skinny skis slide.

This creature is well known as the Eastern Snow Snake. It has been the cause of many bruised skiers' body and ego. It lies in wait along the trail and by wrapping itself about the ankles causes the skier to briefly gain air, only to come tumbling back to earth - usually not feet first.

Unlike its western counterpart that inhabits only powder snow, the Eastern Snow Snake has adapted itself in such a way that it can slither across icy terrain without losing its grip. Its underside is not unlike a radial tread on an all weather tire.

So the next time you take a header while gliding over the snow take a quick look around - you may be the first to actually have visual contact with the dreaded Snow Snake.

EASTERN SNOW SNAKE

CHAPTER FIVE

WAITSFIELD - WARREN

Although the Waitsfield - Warren area appears to be dominated by the alpine ski scene, it is a hotbed of nordic activity as well. There are four ski touring centers in the valley, and as you will see reading through this chapter, there are also many opportunities for backcountry skiing.

If you do both alpine and nordic skiing, you will find this valley to be a great place to take a ski vacation. Sugarbush, Sugarbush North, and Mad River Glen are the alpine areas, and the cross-country areas are all listed in this guide. Accommodations range from charming country inns to luxurious lodges and condominiums. There are many nice shops and restaurants as well.

Waitsfield is home for the Mad River Canoe Company, one of the country's leading producers of recreational and racing canoes. Obviously tourism is the main industry here, with timber production and farming contributing to the local economy as well.

The valley is flanked on the west and east by mountains. The Mad River, one of Vermont's most popular for canoeing and kayaking in spring, flows north through the center of the valley.

It is a picturesque area and many of the trails included in this chapter will afford you some magnificent views of it while skiing.

CHAPTER FIVE

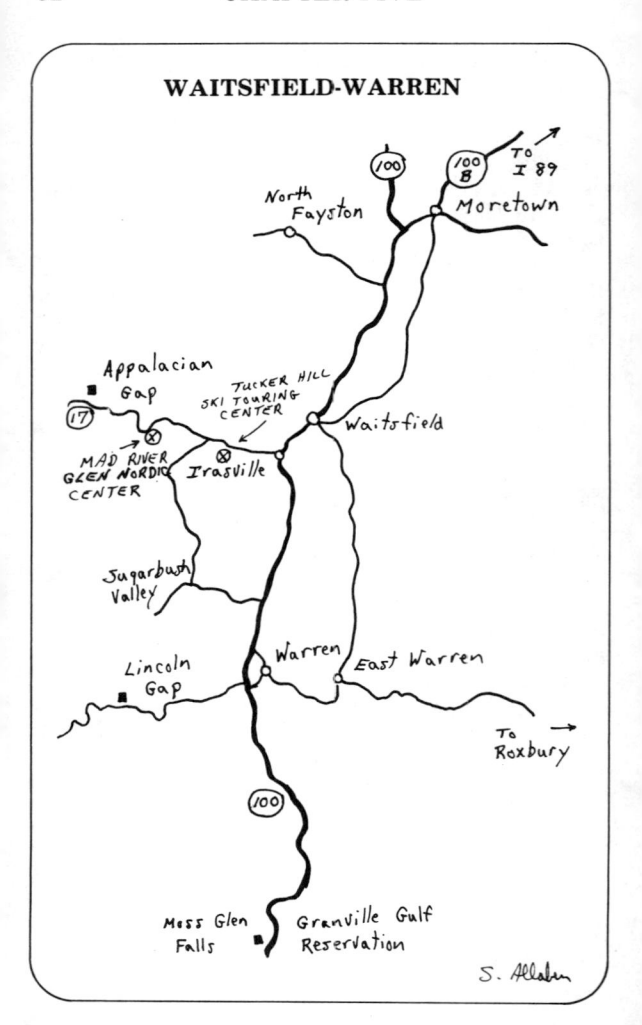

TUCKER HILL SKI TOURING CENTER

RATING: **Easiest/More Difficult/Most Difficult**
TYPE: **Fee/Groomed**
LENGTH: **35 km**
MAP: **Available at the center**
ELEVATION: **1,000' - 1,900'**

Situated in the scenic Mad River Valley, Tucker Hill's trail system is designed primarily for intermediate or better skiers. Some beginner trails are offered here, but a better system is located at a second location (see Mad River Glen Nordic Center -page 94). The trails pass through woodland and open meadows with fine views of the surrounding mountains.

The touring center is based at Tucker Hill Lodge, a beautiful country inn. The center offers rental equipment, instruction, dining and lodging. It is located on a hillside on Route 17.

For further information contact:
Tucker Hill Ski Touring Center
Box 146G
Waitsfield, Vermont 05673

TUCKER HILL S.T.C. - RECOMMENDED TRAIL: TUCKER HILL TO SUGARBUSH INN

RATING: **More Difficult**
LENGTH: **10 km**
TIME: **3-4 Hours**

This route begins at Tucker Hill Lodge and ends at the Sugarbush Inn. Unless you are skiing the route round trip, you will have to leave a car at both ends.

The trail starts by following the Harris Hill Trail to one of three connectors that join with the Sugarbush Inn Trail. The Harris Hill Trail climbs steadily through evergreens and after crossing Harris Hill Road becomes more gradual. All three of the connectors are uphill.

After joining the main trail to Sugarbush Inn the route follows a wide logging road through stands of pine, birch and beech. The trail becomes a lot easier once you reach the Sugar Run Condominiums. It then crosses a beaver pond and joins the Sugarbush Touring Center trails which lead to your final destination, Sugarbush Inn.

MAD RIVER GLEN NORDIC CENTER
RATING: **Easiest/More Difficult**
TYPE: **Fee/Groomed**
LENGTH: **25 km**
MAP: **Available at the center**
ELEVATION: **1,000' - 1,900'**

Operated by the Tucker Hill Ski Touring Center people, Mad River Glen Nordic is located at the Mad River Barn on Route 17 north of Tucker Hill. The trail system consists of beginner and intermediate trails. This is also the entry point to the Hemlock Hill area, where a virtual maze of logging roads exist (see Hemlock Hill Page 95).

The center offers rentals, instruction, a ski shop, lodging, food service and night skiing. This is also the headquarters of the Dick Hall Ski School, which offers the most comprehensive telemark instruction program in Vermont. Telemark instruction is given on the slopes of nearby Mad River Glen ski area.

For further information contact:
Mad River Glen Nordic Center
Box 146G
Waitsfield, Vermont 05673

WAITSFIELD-WARREN

AUSTIN BROOK TRAIL

RATING: **Easiest/More Difficult**
TYPE: **Forest Road**
LENGTH: **8 km (Round trip)**
TIME: **2-3 Hours**
MAP: **Warren and Lincoln (USFS)**
ELEVATION: **1,100' - 1,900'**

The Austin Brook trail is a Forest Service road which joins Route 100 at the upper end of the Granville Gulf Reservation south of Warren. It is a wide road, and although there are some fairly steep pitches along the route, a competent novice can handle it. There are parking facilities on the east side of Route 100 just below the trail head.

The trail begins by crossing the Mad River next to Route 100. It heads west climbing gradually through mixed hardwoods and some conifers. As it comes closer to the brook it climbs more steeply until reaching an elevation of 1,800'. From this point on the climb is more gradual again until the road dead ends at Stetson Brook.

There are several bridge crossings along the way, and some nice views through the woods to the north. Return by the same route and expect to gather some speed on the steeper downhills.

HEMLOCK HILL

RATING: **Easiest/More Difficult/Most Difficult**
TYPE: **Logging Roads**
LENGTH: **30 km**
MAP: **Mount Ellen (USFS)**
ELEVATION: **1,200' - 2,900'**

Hemlock Hill is a large expanse of privately owned land used for commercial timber production.

It is literally laced with good logging roads with sturdy bridges over all stream crossings. It is located next to the Mad River Glen Nordic Center and many of the roads are being incorporated into the center's trail system. Therefore, skiers should check in at the Mad River Glen Nordic Center for information about skiing in the area. Because the extensive system of roads in the Hemlock Hill area is not mapped, you may wish to hire a guide from one of the two local cross-country centers (Mad River Glen Nordic and Tucker Hill).

This area has exceptional glade skiing for telemark skiers with easy access to high elevations. There are some great views from the higher elevations. If you are skiing in the Waitsfield area, you should plan to spend a day skiing Hemlock Hill.

STARK MOUNTAIN RIDGE TRAIL

RATING: **More Difficult**
TYPE: **Wilderness**
LENGTH: **8-10 km**
TIME: **3-4 Hours**
MAP: **Mount Ellen (USFS)**
ELEVATION: **1,500' - 4,000'**

This spectacular trail follows the Long Trail from the summit of the Mad River Glen ski area to Sugarbush North ski area. If skied north to south it is nearly all downhill. Your downhill technique had better be in top form as you will be skiing down the alpine ski trails at Sugarbush North.

To get to the beginning of the route, take the right hand chairlift at Mad River Glen to the top (single ride tickets can be purchased). When you get off the chairlift turn left and follow the Long Trail, which is marked with white blazes (sometimes not visible). This route follows the spine of the ridge, so there is no way you can get off course.

When you get off the chairlift turn left and follow the Long Trail. The trail is level at first and soon reaches the Theron Dean Shelter. There is a sharp climb up here to level terrain along the ridge where the trail will again climb for a short distance. Coming out of the woods the trail will now follow the Fall Line ski trail to the top of another chairlift. Beyond the chairlift the trail then follows another ski trail for a short distance and then continues once again along the ridge.

At the junction of the Barton Trail you can follow this short spur east to Glen Ellen Lodge, a log structure that sleeps 8-10 people. At this point there are some spectacular views to the east, with the Presidential Range of the White Mountains in New Hampshire far in the distance.

After passing the Jerusalem Trail, which heads west, the trail winds back and forth along the ridge until it reaches the Sugarbush North chairlift. At this point you begin your descent to the base lodge in the valley below by following the easiest ski trails down.

This route offers many spectacular views in all directions. It is probably the most scenic cross-country ski route in the central Vermont region.

KEW HILL TRAIL
RATING: **More Difficult**
TYPE: **Forest Road**
LENGTH: **6 km (Round trip)**
TIME: **3 Hours**
MAP: **Waitsfield (USFS)**
ELEVATION: **800' - 1,500'**

Although not a long tour, this route is worth trying, because it leads to a cabin from which there is a great view across the Mad River valley to the Northfield Mountains.

The beginning of the trail is at the point where plowing ends on the first road to the left off Route 17 just after you turn off Route 100.

The trail climbs steeply the first 1½ km, and then climbs more gradually through a section of Camels Hump State Forest. It levels off at 1,500' and then drops down gradually crossing two brooks. After the second brook the trail climbs again gradually and then levels off to the cabin. Return by the same route.

NORTHFIELD MOUNTAINS TRAIL
RATING: **Easiest/More Difficult**
TYPE: **Forest Roads**
LENGTH: **8-10 km**
MAP: **Waitsfield (USFS)**
ELEVATION: **1,100' - 1,600'**

Also known as the Scragg Mountain area, this route interconnects a series of old town roads and fields and may also be used by snowmobiles. There are many more kilometers of roads and trails to explore in this area other than what is described here.

The best place to park is at the end of Palmer Hill Road. To get there cross the covered bridge in Waitsfield, and past the cemetery bear left at the fork. Palmer Hill Road is the second right beyond this point.

Where the plowing stops, begin skiing on the unplowed road heading east. The trail climbs easily through hardwoods until it forks north and south. Take the north fork. The trail continues on a very gradual downhill, crossing several small streams. It will then connect with another road that goes off to the left (north west). Continue in a north easterly direction through fields and a stand of trees with a trail through the middle. The trail then connects with another road to the west. Continue on to the northeast along a logging road, which leads to an intersection of another road. Go straight ahead through more fields. This will lead to yet another road, which eventually ends up in Moretown Common.

The trail passes to the east of Mount Waitsfield, and to the east just off the trail near this point there is a log cabin. It contains a log book, which passers-by can sign.

Not too much further on, the trail will widen and eventually reach a point where the road is plowed. At this point you should turn around and follow the same route back. There is a short cut on the way back, which you can follow by taking the last branch road to the west, crossing Pine Brook. Ski down this across the brook and when you reach the fields on the south side of the road, cut across them to another road that leads back to the starting point.

FINN BASIN

RATING: **More Difficult**
TYPE: **Fee/Partially Groomed**
LENGTH: **10-15 km**
MAP: **Mount Ellen (USFS)**
ELEVATION: **1,000' - 1,600'**

The Finn Basin is part of the Mad River Glen Nordic Center's trail system. It is a remote basin that is nestled against the east side of the mountains, and as a result receives an exceptional amount of snowfall due to a dumping effect when storms come in from the west.

In the basin is a small valley with beaver ponds and a large wooded bowl with steep hillsides. There

100 CHAPTER FIVE

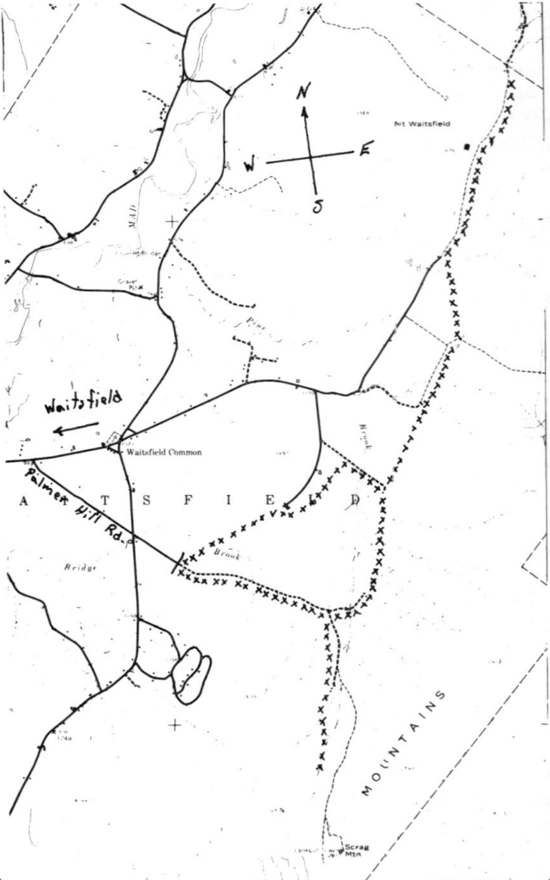

is an access trail leading into this area that is maintained by the touring center. There is easily a day's worth of skiing here for the more experienced skier seeking a wilderness-type setting.

BRAGG HILL

RATING: **Easiest/More Difficult**
TYPE: **Logging Road**
LENGTH: **8-10 km**
TIME: **2-4 Hours**
MAP: **Waitsfield**
ELEVATION: **1,100' - 1,900'**

The Bragg Hill area is just outside of Waitsfield and is accessible by following Bragg Hill Road off of Route 100. The turn off is the first left after you go north past Route 17. There is a turnaround at the end of the plowed road where limited parking is available.

There is an old road that heads north about 3½ km to a point where it meets a plowed road. You can ski out and back on this route, which is fairly level mixed with some gentle up and down. The old road is also used by local snowmobilers, so it is most apt to be packed out.

If you are competent with a map and compass, there is good skiing by bushwacking your way back around the east side of the ridge that lies to the east of the road. You will encounter other old logging roads in this section, some of which you can utilize on your trip back. I have indicated a general route on the map, however, because there is no clear route, you will have to refer to your compass and map continuously.

OLE'S CROSS COUNTRY CENTER

RATING: **Easiest/More Difficult/Most Difficult**
TYPE: **Fee/Groomed**
LENGTH: **74 km**
MAP: **Available at the center**
ELEVATION: **1,200' - 2,450'**

This center is located at the airport in Warren and offers instruction, guided tours, rental equipment, a cafe, changing rooms and showers.

The trail system is partially groomed and is situated in wooded as well as open terrain. There is a wide variety of trail types here, from wide, tracked trails, to primitive backcountry skiing routes.

For further information contact:
Ole's Cross Country Center
Airport Road
Warren, Vermont 05674

SUGARBUSH INN SKI TOURING CENTER

RATING: **Easiest/More Difficult/Most Difficult**
TYPE: **Fee/Groomed**
LENGTH: **60 km**
MAP: **Available at the center**
ELEVATION: **1,300' - 1,900'**

Located on the access road to Sugarbush Ski Area, the Sugarbush Inn Ski Touring Center is a complete skiing facility, offering rentals, instruction, lodging, meals, and an extensive trail system.

The trails follow the Sugarbush golf course, as well as old roads through open hardwoods, and fields. The Slide, which is a wide trail on a logging road, leads to Sugarbush North Ski Area. The area's trail system also connects with the nearby Tucker Hill Ski Touring Center.

For further information contact:
 Sugarbush Inn Ski Touring Center
 Warren, Vermont 05674

KNOLL FARM COUNTRY INN

A quiet farm-inn where you can X-C ski or snowshoe through high pastures and peaceful woods, eat family, farm-grown meals, and sit by a warm wood stove.

Enjoy a country winter with us!

Bragg Hill Rd., Waitsfield, VT 05673
(802) 496-3939

CHAPTER FIVE

Millbrook.... a country inn

Six beautifully decorated guest rooms; relaxed atmosphere. Cross-country skiing from our back door. Our guests dine by the fireplace in our romantic, candlelit restaurant. Enjoy ordering such specialties as handrolled pasta, fine veal, shrimp, and homemade desserts from our varied menu. Your first visit won't be your last. Joan and Thom Gorman, Innkeepers.

RFD Box 62, Waitsfield, VT 05673 (802) 496-2405

Mountain View Inn

RFD Box 48A, Waitsfield, VT 05673
802/496-2426

An old Vermont farmhouse lovingly decorated and furnished with heirloom antiques. Homecooked meals served family style around a large pine harvest table. On the Tucker Hill-Mad River Barn x-country ski trail. Seven rooms with private baths. Capacity 14. Owners: Fred and Suzy Spencer.

Open Year Round

WAITSFIELD-WARREN

Mad River Glen Nordic Center
&
Tucker Hill Ski Touring Center

Ski tour 60 km. of groomed trails that link country inns, gentle meadows, and rolling woodlands. Certified ski school • complete sales and rentals • telemark instructional program • back country tours • night skiing. Quaint hospitable accommodations provide the charm and restfulness of a traditional New England community. Nestled in the Green Mountains with the vitality and attractions of a major resort.

RT. 17, BOX 146, WAITSFIELD, VERMONT 05673
(802) 496-3203

Write for a free brochure

CHAPTER FIVE

Tucker Hill Lodge

IN THE SUGARBUSH/MAD RIVER VALLEY, VERMONT

A Very Special Country Inn
and Restaurant Noted for Outstanding
Cuisine and Gracious Hospitality.

X-C Center on premises (see ad)
Special Ski Touring Packages

RFD 1 BOX 147, WAITSFIELD, VERMONT 05673
802-496-3983 or 1-800-451-4580

NATURE NOTES

FISHER

FISHER

The fisher is a dark brown to nearly black furbearing member of the weasel family. It is between 33 to 40 inches long, including the 13-15 inch bushy tail, and weighs between 3 to 12 pounds. Although active day and night, it is not an animal you will encounter very often while skiing.

The fisher feeds on small mammals, carrion, fruit, and birds. It is one of the only predators that feeds on porcupines.

Sometimes called a fisher cat, this animal is neither a fisher or a cat. Its fondness for porcupines has been its salvation, as otherwise it would have become extinct some years ago from trapping. Its pelt would bring as much as $300.00 in the 1920's. Due to dwindling populations, several states, including Vermont, began to protect the fisher in an effort to check the rapid increase of the destructive porcupine.

The most interesting aspect of the fisher is its reproductive process. After mating, the fertilized eggs develop into embryos and then stop growing and remain dormant in the female for nine to ten months. In the following January or February the embryos begin to develop until the kits are born sometime between late February and April. This reproductive cycle is known as discontinuous development, giving the fisher a 51 week gestation period - the longest of any North American mammal.

CHAPTER SIX

MONTPELIER - RANDOLPH

This series of ski trail guides wouldn't be complete if I didn't somehow figure a way to include Vermont's state capital. As you will see by reading on, even here you will find cross-country skiing facilities. Legislators and bureaucrats like to ski too.

For a state capital, Montpelier is a plain, yet gracious town. The gold domed capitol building and other government buildings all face the main thoroughfare. The Vermont Historical Society has a museum just down the street from the capitol in a restored Victorian building. Here you will find a wealth of Vermont history.

The countryside in the Montpelier - Randolph area is very picturesque, with rolling hills of open farm land and forests. It is ideally suited for cross-country skiing, but because there is very little public land, as in other parts of central Vermont, there are limited opportunities for the general public. However, what there is you will find very gratifying.

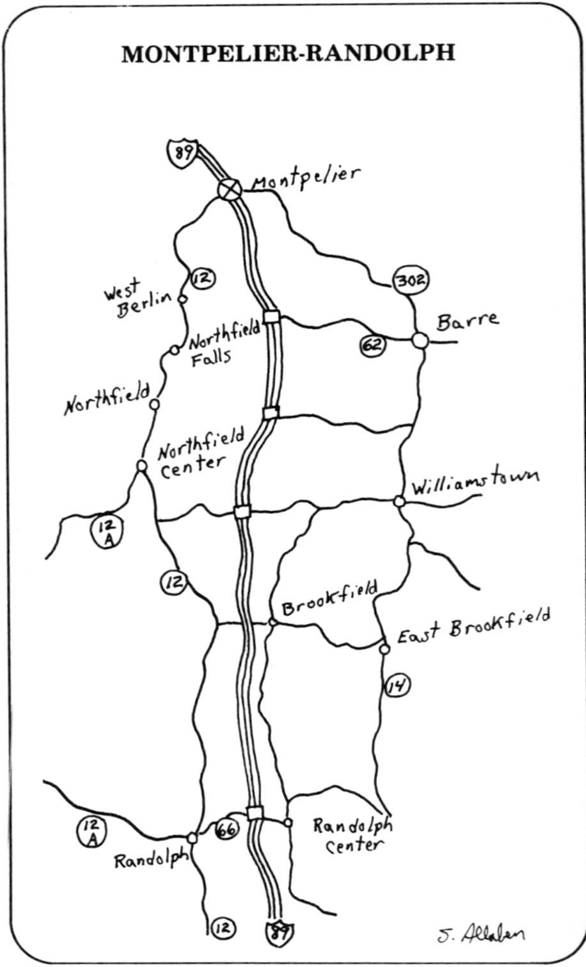

CHAPTER SIX

MONTPELIER-RANDOLPH

MONTPELIER ELKS SKI TOURING CENTER

RATING: **Easiest/More Difficult**
TYPE: **Fee/Groomed**
LENGTH: **10 km**
MAP: **Available at the center**
ELEVATION: **800' - 850'**

This cross-country ski center is located on Route 2 at the golf course of the Montpelier Elks Club. The area is well suited for families and beginners, as the trails follow gently rolling terrain over and around the golf course. It is also an excellent trail system for racers or physical fitness buffs to train on.

Facilities include a restaurant and bar and showers.

For further information contact:
Warren Kitzmiller
Onion River Sports
20 Langdon St.
Montpelier, Vermont 05602

HUBBARD PARK

RATING: **More Difficult**
TYPE: **Municipal Park**
LENGTH: **8 km**
ELEVATION: **600' - 850'**

This 300 acre park is located in Montpelier center. It is rather hilly and the trails are not groomed or maintained. However, it is wooded and scenic and open every day from 9:00 until sunset. It is not well suited for beginners due to the extreme variations in terrain.

GREEN MOUNTAIN SKI TOURING CENTER

RATING: **Easiest/More Difficult/Most Difficult**
TYPE: **Fee/Groomed**
LENGTH: **35 km**
MAP: **Available at the center**
ELEVATION: **850' - 1,450'**

This touring center is located at the Green Mountain Stock Farm in Randolph on over 1,000 acres of pasture land and forests. The terrain is varied, with gently rolling hills as well as stretches of flat trails suitable for the beginner. Scenic views are numerous, and there is even an active beaver pond within the trail system.

The center offers instruction, rental equipment, groomed trails, lodging and meals.

For further information contact:
  Green Mountain Ski Touring Center
  Randolph, Vermont 05060

GREEN TRAILS SKI TOURING CENTER

RATING: **Easiest/More Difficult/Most Difficult**
TYPE: **Fee/Groomed**
LENGTH: **40 km**
MAP: **Available at the center**
ELEVATION: **1,132' - 1,572'**

Located at the Green Trails Inn, the center has rental equipment, a ski shop, lodging, and meals. The trail system follows rolling terrain through hardwood and conifer forests, as well as open meadows with highland vistas, over frozen lakes and ponds and a beaver bog. One can ski to nearby

MONTPELIER-RANDOLPH

400 acre Allis State Park where there is a firetower from the top of which are fantastic views.

For further information contact:
  Green Trails Inn and Ski Touring Center
  Brookfield, Vermont 05036

GREEN MOUNTAIN NATIONAL FOREST

The Green Mountain National Forest is composed of over 250,000 acres extending from the Massachusetts border to nearly 100 miles North. It is divided into three districts; Middlebury, Rochester, and Manchester. All trails in this guide that are within National Forest boundaries are in the first two districts. The dividing line for the two districts is the Appalachian Trail.

The U.S. Forest Service manages this public land for the purposes of timber production, wildlife habitat, recreation, and water resources under the principle of multiple use.

All of the Green Mountain National Forest is open to cross-country skiing, although some areas are not well suited. Because of ongoing timber harvesting operations throughout the forest, seemingly unlimited miles of logging roads have been constructed and are well suited for cross-country skiing.

If you wish to obtain updated information regarding any part of the National Forest covered in this guide contact:

Middlebury District
Green Mountain National Forest
Route 7
Middlebury, Vermont 05753

Rochester District
Green Mountain National Forest
Route 100
Rochester, Vermont 05767

GUIDE SERVICE

Some of Vermont's finest cross country skiing is found in remote areas of the Green Mountain National Forest. Here you will find active beaver ponds, remote ponds and streams, scenic vistas with nothing in sight but forests, mountain meadows and high mountain peaks. Unfortunately for many, these treasures are beyond reach, for one must be competent in backcountry travel and use of a map and compass in order to reap the rewards of such ski travel.

Luckily, though, for the skier with proficient skiing skills, but lacking in knowledge of backcountry travel, there are a few individuals in central Vermont who employ themselves as backcountry guides. Under their guidance you too can get into God's country on cross country skis.

Besides the individuals listed below, some of the commercial cross country ski areas offer guide service as well.

Ann Mausolff
Ski Tours of Vermont
RFD 1-G
Chester, Vermont 05143

Dean Mendell
Nordic Adventures
Box 115 RD 1
Rochester, Vermont 05767

Dick Hall and Rob Center
Mad River Glen Nordic Center
Box 146 RD 1
Waitsfield, Vermont 05673

INN TO INN SKIING

To truly experience cross country skiing in Vermont to its fullest potential, one must try inn to inn skiing. It is a vacation that combines the enjoyment of skiing through the scenic Vermont countryside with dining and lodging at some of the area's loveliest country inns.

Both guided and self-guided programs are offered in the central region. A day's activity includes several hours of skiing backcountry trails and unplowed roads with a break for a scrumptuous trail lunch. Some programs entail skiing from one inn directly to the other, or combining travel on skis with automobile shuttling for those who wish to limit the amount of kilometers skied in a day.

Below are the addresses of businesses that specialize in inn to inn cross country ski tours.

Nordic Adventures
Box 115 RD 1
Rochester, Vermont 05767

Ski Tours of Vermont
RFD 1-G
Chester, Vermont 05143

Inn To Inn Tours
RD 3-G
Brandon, Vermont 05733

REFERENCES

Johnson, Charles W., The Nature of Vermont, The University Press of New England, Hanover, New Hampshire.

Burt, William Henry and Grossenheider, Richard Phillip, A Field Guide To The Mammals, Peterson Field Guide Series, Houghton Mifflin Company, Boston.

Tanner, Ogden, The New England Wilds, American Wilderness/Time-Life Books, New York.

Reilly, Edgar M. Jr., The Audubon Illustrated Handbook of American Birds, McGraw-Hill Book Co., New York.

Line, Les, The Audubon Society Book of Wild Birds, Harry N. Abrans, Inc., New York.

Green Mountain Club, Guide Book of the Long Trail, Montpelier, Vermont.

MAP RESOURCES

U.S. Forest Service
Route 7
Middlebury, Vermont

U.S. Forest Service
Federal Building
Rutland, Vermont

U.S. Forest Service
Route 100
Rochester, Vermont

Benn Burry Shop
Merchants Row
Rutland, Vermont

Capital Stationers
Main Street
Montpelier, Vermont

HOSPITALS AND MEDICAL CENTERS

Randolph - Gifford Memorial Hospital
Hanover, N.H. - Dartmouth Hitchcock Medical Center
Rutland - Rutland Hospital
Middlebury - Porter Medical Center
Woodstock - Ottauquechee Health Center
Waitsfield - Mad River Valley Health Center

INDEX OF TRAILS

Austin Brook Trail	95
Beaver Meadows Trail	58
Bingo Brook Trail	73
Blueberry Hill Ski Touring Center	48
Bragg Hill	101
Breadloaf Ski Touring Center	55
Caryl Brook To Michigan Brook Trail	85
Chittenden Brook Trail	80
Churchill House Ski Touring Center	51
Cortina Inn To Tulip Tree Inn Trail	6
Dragon Brook Trail	59
Elbow Road Trail	15
Finn Basin	99
Forest Road 59	58
Granville Gulf Trail	84
Green Mountain Ski Touring Center	112
Green Trails Ski Touring Center	112
Hancock Branch Brook Trail	71
Hemlock Hill	95
Hubbard Park	111
Kedron Valley Inn Ski Touring Center	37
Kew Hill Trail	97
Liberty Hill	77
Long Trail - Brandon Gap	50
Mad River Glen Nordic Center	94
Mendon Brook Trail	10
Middle Road Trail	51
Montpelier Elks Ski Touring Center	111
Mount Tom Trail System	29
Mountain Meadows Ski Touring Center	3
Mountain Top Ski Touring Center	4
Natural Turnpike	53
Norske Trail	52
North Pond Trail	83
Northfield Mountains Trail	98

INDEX OF TRAILS

Ole's Cross Country Center	102
Quechee Lakes Touring Trails	36
Pine Brook Trail	76
Puss And Kill Brook Trail	13
Robert Frost Farm	54
Rutland City Forest	5
Skyline Trail	31
South Pond Trail	16
South Pond Trail To Elbow Road	16
Stark Mountain Ridge Trail	96
Sugarbush Inn Ski Touring Center	102
Texas Gap Trail	71
Townsend Brook Trail	84
Trail Head Ski Touring Center	78
Tucker Hill Ski Touring Center	93
Wilderness Trails Ski School and Touring Center	36
Woodstock Ski Touring Center	28

INDEX OF
LODGING, RESTAURANTS, & SHOPS

Art Bennett's Sport Shop	xii
Blueberry Hill Ski Touring Center	64
Brandon Inn	66
Brandon Motor Lodge	68
Charity's	24
Chipman Inn	63
Churchill House	62
Hogge Penny	23
Huntington House	89
Inn At Long Trail	21
Inn At Mt. Ascutney	39
Inn At Weathersfield	42
Kedron Valley Inn	38
Knoll Farm	103
Long Run Inn	67
Lothlorien	22
Mad River Glen Nordic Center	105
Millbrook Lodge	104
Mountain Meadows Ski Touring Center	22
Mountain Top Ski Touring Center And Inn	20
Mountain View Inn	104
Pico Bavarian Haus	23
Pittsfield Inn	89
Punderson Agency Real Estate	24
Quechee Inn At Marshland Farm	38
Red Clover Inn	21
Rumbleseat Restaurant	40
Salomon	113
Skihaus	63
Tucker Hill Lodge	106
Tucker Hill Ski Touring Center	105
Valley View Motel	43
Waybury Inn	65
Woodstock Inn And Resort	41

The Perfect Cure for

Cabin Fever

Join the VERMONT NATURAL RESOURCES COUNCIL!

We promise to remind you of all that good stuff under the snow, like clean lakes and rivers, and farmland waiting for spring planting.

And we hope you'll feel better when you're doing something to help protect it.

A membership contribution to VNRC is a boost for the environment that makes Vermont so enjoyable.

Write us for a free copy of our brochure, annual report, or our latest newsletter, the VERMONT ENVIRONMENTAL REPORT.

Or send a check for one of the following types of membership to the address below:

Individual - $15
Family - $20
Student - $5
Fixed/Limited Income - $6
Business - $25, $50, or $100

Vermont Natural Resources Council
7 MAIN STREET THE OLD DEPOT
MONTPELIER, VERMONT 05602

VERMONT INSTITUTE OF NATURAL SCIENCE

woodstock vermont 05091

At the Vermont Institute of Natural Science we believe that if a harmony between man and his environment is possible anywhere, it is here in Vermont.

VINS is a non-profit membership organization supported solely by memberships and private contributions. Since 1972, our programs have traveled throughout the state from our headquarters in Woodstock, educating Vermonters of all ages. We also conduct important research on the birds of Vermont.

Write for a copy of our brochure or our latest newsletter. Your membership actively supports environmental education for all the people of Vermont.

NOTES

NOTES

NOTES

NOTES